# The Doolittle Raid 1942

America's first strike back at Japan

D1560602

Campaign • 156

# The Doolittle Raid 1942

America's first strike back at Japan

Clayton K S Chun • Illustrated by Howard Gerrard

First published in 2006 by Osprey Publishing

Midland House, West Way, Botley, Oxford OX2 0PH, UK

443 Park Avenue South, New York, NY 10016, USA

E-mail: info@ospreypublishing.com

ISBN-10: 1-84176-918-5

ISBN-13: 978-1-84176-918-9

Design: Black Spot

Index by Alison Worthington

Cartography: The Map Studio

3D BEVs: Black Spot

Originated by PPS-Grasmere, Leeds, UK

Printed and bound in China through Worldprint

Typeset in Helvetica Neue and ITC New Baskerville

06 07 08 09 10   11 10 9 8 7 6 5 4 3 2

A CIP catalog record for this book is available from the British Library.

For a catalog of all books published by Osprey please contact:

NORTH AMERICA

Osprey Direct, C/o Random House Distribution Center, 400 Hahn Road, Westminster, MD 21157

E-mail: info@ospreydirect.com

ALL OTHER REGIONS

Osprey Direct UK, P.O. Box 140, Wellingborough, Northants, NN8 2FA, UK

E-mail: info@ospreydirect.co.uk

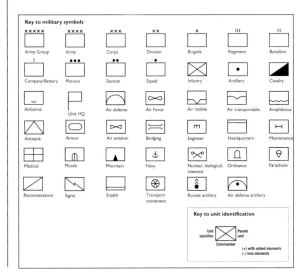

# Image credits

The photos in this book are from the collections of the US Navy, Air Force, Army, and the US National Archives and Records Administration (NARA) in College Park, MD.

# Acknowledgments

I want to thank the individuals who supported me in writing this book. Mickey Russell from the Air Force Historical Research Agency, Maxwell AFB, AL provided superb help in getting me many files on the Doolittle Raid. Robert E. Schnare, Library Director of the US Naval War College, Newport, RI obtained many logs for me from ships involved in the mission. The staff from the Military History Institute, Carlisle Barracks, PA were always willing to lend a hand in this project. My editor Nikolai Bogdanovic kept me on the straight and narrow throughout. Finally, I want to thank my family for their understanding and patience.

# Abbreviations

**AAF rank abbreviations**

| | |
|---|---|
| Col | Colonel |
| LTC | Lieutenant Colonel |
| Maj | Major |
| Capt | Captain |
| 1Lt | First Lieutenant |
| 2Lt | Second Lieutenant |
| M/Sgt | Master Sergeant |
| T/Sgt | Technical Sergeant |
| S/Sgt | Staff Sergeant |
| Sgt | Sergeant |
| Cpl | Corporal |

**Navy rank abbreviations**

| | |
|---|---|
| CAPT | Captain |
| CDR | Commander |
| LCDR | Lieutenant Commander |
| LT | Lieutenant |
| LT(JG) | Lieutenant (Junior Grade) |
| ENS | Ensign |

# Artist's note

Readers may care to note that the original paintings from which the color plates in this book were prepared are available for private sale. The Publishers retain all reproduction copyright whatsoever. All enquiries should be addressed to:

Howard Gerrard, 11 Oaks Road, Tenterden, Kent, TN30 6RD, UK

The Publishers regret that they can enter into no correspondence upon this matter.

# Linear measurements

Distances, ranges, and dimensions are given in the contemporary US system of inches, feet, yards, and statute miles rather than metric:

| | |
|---|---|
| feet to meters: | multiply feet by 0.3048 |
| yards to meters: | multiply yards by 0.9144 |
| miles to kilometers: | multiply miles by 1.6093 |

# CONTENTS

# JAPANESE CONQUEST OF THE PACIFIC, DECEMBER 1941–APRIL 1942

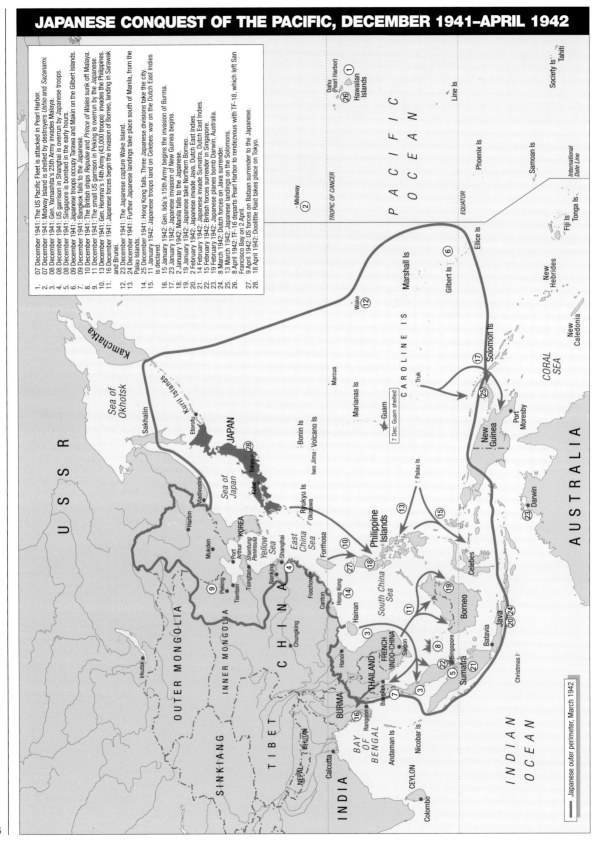

1. 07 December 1941: The US Pacific Fleet is attacked in Pearl Harbor.
2. 07 December 1941: Midway Island is shelled by destroyers *Ushio* and *Sazanami*.
3. 08 December 1941: Gen. Yamashita's 25th Army invades Malaya.
4. 08 December 1941: US garrison in Shanghai is overrun by Japanese troops.
5. 08 December 1941: Singapore is bombed in the early hours.
6. 09 December 1941: Japanese troops occupy Tarawa and Makin on the Gilbert Islands.
7. 09 December 1941: Bangkok falls to the Japanese.
8. 10 December 1941: The British ships *Repulse* and *Prince of Wales* sunk off Malaya.
9. 11 December 1941: The Japanese garrison in Peking is overrun by the Japanese.
10. 13 December 1941: The small US garrison in Peking is overrun by the Japanese.
11. 16 December 1941: Gen. Homma's 14th Army (43,000 troops) invades the Philippines.
11. 16 December 1941: Japanese forces begin the invasion of Borneo, landing in Sarawak and Brunei.
12. 23 December 1941: The Japanese capture Wake Island.
13. 24 December 1941: Further Japanese landings take place south of Manila, from the Palau Islands.
14. 25 December 1941: Hong Kong falls. Three Japanese divisions take the city.
15. 11 January 1942: Japanese troops land on Celebes: war on the Dutch East Indies is declared.
16. 15 January 1942: Gen. Iida's 15th Army begins the invasion of Burma.
17. 23 January 1942: Japanese invasion of New Guinea begins.
18. 19 January 1942: Manila falls to the Japanese.
19. 19 January 1942: Japanese take Northern Borneo.
20. 01 February 1942: Japanese invade Java, Dutch East Indies.
21. 14 February 1942: Japanese invade Sumatra, Dutch East Indies.
22. 15 February 1942: British forces surrender in Singapore.
23. 19 February 1942: Japanese planes bomb Darwin, Australia.
24. 8 March 1942: Dutch forces on Java surrender.
25. 13 March 1942: Japanese landings on the Solomons.
26. 8 April 1942: TF-16 departs Pearl Harbor to rendezvous with TF-18, which left San Francisco Bay on 2 April.
27. 9 April 1942: US forces on Bataan surrender to the Japanese.
28. 18 April 1942: Doolittle Raid takes place on Tokyo.

Japanese outer perimeter, March 1942

6

# INTRODUCTION

The Doolittle Raid demonstrated many characteristics of warfare that leaders today desire, but rarely see. The April 18, 1942 attack on Tokyo and surrounding areas used joint military forces; involved relatively few resources; was organized and executed in a phenomenally short period of time; achieved surprise; allowed commanders to accept risk; forced innovative planning; and the results had a significant strategic effect. This daring attack was one of the most famous raids in World War II, one that changed the course of events in the Pacific.

In early 1942, the strategic picture for the Allies was very bleak. In the Pacific Theater, the United States, the British Empire, and the Netherlands had been in continual retreat since December 7, 1941. The United States had surrendered major areas of the Philippines, lost Guam, admitted defeat at Wake Island, and was preparing for the worst in Hawaii and on the West Coast. American air, land, and sea forces could not stop the Japanese, and the nation seemed paralyzed by the prospects of major theater campaigns from Europe to the Pacific. The American public, while stung by the events in Pearl Harbor, faced major sacrifices to gather the men and *matériel* needed to fight a global war. The national leadership in Washington tried every method to mobilize the resources and the people's will to defeat the Axis powers.

The United States was not the only nation facing defeat. British military units in Hong Kong, Malaya, and later Singapore were brushed aside by advancing Japanese forces. Britain was fully engaged in Europe and the Middle East; another major theater would tax its strained military and populace. Defenders in the Dutch East Indies crumbled, and it seemed that Australia was ripe for conquest. The Japanese poured into areas throughout the Southwest Pacific. Although China had been at war with Japan for years, she faced occupation and growing Japanese military expansion throughout the country. The Soviet Union, which had previously wrestled with the Japanese, signed a non-aggression pact in April 1941, while fully engaged with the Germans. Japan was also entrenched in French Indo-China and continued to control its vassal state, Korea. The United States' strategic position seemed hardly enviable and the Japanese appeared unstoppable.

President Franklin Delano Roosevelt, who had revived the American people's spirit and lifted the nation out of economic depression, was faced with a new war that required extraordinary leadership and skill to win. Although he had prepared the nation for war by increasing military spending and enlarging force structure, he now had to regain the public's confidence to overcome the recent string of military disasters. Without the will of the people, the United States would have a difficult time marshaling the proper level of support and performance from Americans in or out of uniform. The military, economic, and political

elements of national power would suffer severe strain if events were not reversed. The American will to energize industry, agriculture, and the military to become an effective force against the Axis powers had to be fostered carefully.

The Doolittle Raid was a masterful combination of planning, daring, and execution. Throughout the raid's planning, a joint perspective of the military operation was used. Army and Navy resources were used to overcome shortfalls and push innovative thinking to fruition. This operation foreshadowed, in some respects, future joint Army–Navy operations in the Pacific, in which combined forces would co-operate to dismantle the Japanese Empire by island-hopping actions throughout the Pacific. Deploying a land-based medium bomber force from an aircraft carrier had never been accomplished before, and such a bold plan required close co-operation, training, and planning.

Acceptance of risk by senior military leadership was also a key part of the raid. The potential loss of a major task force, while limited naval resources maintained the thin defensive line of the United States Pacific Fleet, was not to be taken lightly, nor was the nation's willingness to accept risk. The nation would need to use a significant amount of vital naval forces to launch an attack comprising only 16 bombers. On the face of it, the returns were minimal compared to the risks. A simple cost-benefit in tactical terms would have forced a cancelation of the attack; however, the strategic effect was the key factor. Affecting the enemy's confidence, and shifting the strategic focus for the Japanese, far out-weighed the potential loss of Doolittle's aircraft. Raising the confidence of the United States' populace towards winning the war was another potential benefit. A few daring men willing to take a chance could bring significant rewards for the US.

The strategic effect also demonstrated the value of air power. Earlier advocates of this new aspect of military power had argued that air power

Japanese forces were triumphant throughout Southeast Asia and the Pacific early in the war. Nothing seemed to stand in the way of the Japanese in late 1941. (National Archives)

could create far-ranging influences by attacking critical targets. For example, the destruction of leadership or key industrial areas could cripple a targeted country. Air power also provided a relatively swift and direct strike capability straight to the heart of an enemy, as shown at Pearl Harbor and in the Battle of Britain. An attack on Tokyo and other areas could demonstrate the vulnerability of the Japanese leadership, military, industry, and people and show that their navy and air forces could not defend themselves.

The mood change throughout the United States also helped encourage other activities. For example, individuals began to purchase more war bonds. Rates of production of war *matériel* also increased. These actions not only supported the Pacific Theater campaign, but enhanced America's image as an "Arsenal of Democracy" that offered a lifeline to its European allies.

The Japanese Empire, on the other hand, was near its apex. Japanese advances in the Pacific after World War I included the ceding of the Marshall Islands and other areas from Germany, which reinforced the idea that its imperial rise was no fluke. Japan now controlled a large area of the Central Pacific between Hawaii and the Philippines. It expanded its empire with the occupation of Manchuria and parts of China beginning in 1922, without serious opposition. The League of Nations stood by and watched as Japan took ever bolder steps. When confronted over this, they simply left the organization. World naval powers also included Japan in discussions about naval tonnage and limits on certain types of capital ships. Although restricted in tonnage, the Japanese also negotiated treaty terms that restricted the fortification and strengthening of certain military installations, like Hong Kong and Singapore. This point would help Japan's eventual control of these areas. The Japanese Empire seemed to meet with success at almost every step. The Greater East-Asia Co-Prosperity Sphere had mushroomed from early occupations of parts of China, Korea, and Manchuria to expand south to Malaya and New Guinea and east to Wake Island. The 1941 Japanese steamroller had flattened the Western colonial powers with ease, echoing the success of the previous generation in the Russo-Japanese War of 1904. Tokyo demonstrated its forces were capable of defeating an enemy with modern technology on land and sea.

Japanese success on the battlefield and the negotiating table did not translate necessarily to instant improvements at home. The Japanese people and economy required many types and large quantities of scarce resources. Many of these raw materials were available in Asia, but they were under colonial rule of several countries. Despite having greater military and political influence, through conquest, the growing population and economic needs of the nation required immediate attention. The Japanese failure to ensure resource access was a key vulnerability that other nations could exploit. The unchecked, indefensible conquest of Asian territory was reason enough to limit trade

to Japan. Nations around the world were alarmed as the ambitious Japanese occupied more Asian territory. By the late 1930s, many nations had become more concerned. America and other countries tried to restrict the sale of oil and key materials for various political and economic reasons. The United States also withheld finished products, aiming to stunt Tokyo's economy. American efforts to stop Japanese expansion also included the freezing of assets and the increased sale of war materials and aid to Chiang Kai-shek and the Nationalist forces in China. Russia had also shown its military superiority over Japan in border clashes, and expansion northwards seemed limited. However, when France and the Netherlands fell to Germany, the Japanese looked south to regain access to vital resources like oil, rubber, metals, and foodstuffs. A central question to the Japanese national leadership was how to gain access to resources or end embargoes without spurring the United States or Great Britain into declaring war. Despite this concern, the prospects of avoiding confrontation seemed bleak. The diplomatic means failed, and offensive operations began that ultimately led to Pearl Harbor.

Japanese hopes were for a quick victory that would secure a well-defended perimeter and destroy the United States and Allied capability to dislodge their expansion. The Japanese succeeded, and pushed the Allies towards an outer boundary that did not seem too easy to breach. How could the United States change the strategic environment to allow the nation to regain not only lost territory, but remove any future threat to remaining Allied areas? Was the rest of China, India, Australia, or New Zealand next on the list of conquered countries? Given the limited resources available to a mobilizing United States, what actions could Roosevelt and his military staffs propose? The nation faced sudden disaster, something needed to happen quickly and be of considerable impact. The Doolittle Raid was a way to achieve this.

# CHRONOLOGY

*All times are local.*

## 1941

**December 7** Japan attacks Pearl Harbor and starts military operations against the United States, Britain, and the Netherlands.
**December 8** Japanese forces invade the Philippines and Malaya.
**December 10** Guam, Makin, and Tarawa are invaded and occupied by Japan.
**December 11** Germany and Italy declare war on the United States.
**December 21** Roosevelt calls for a bombing raid against Japan.
**December 22** Start of Arcadia Conference between America and Britain. During the conference US Navy planners develop the initial idea for the Tokyo raid based on a scheme to transport aircraft to North Africa.
**December 23** Wake Island falls to the Japanese after US Marines put up a valiant defense.
**December 25** Japan takes Hong Kong.

## 1942

**January** Japanese Army units invade Burma, and later move north to the Chinese border and threaten India.
**January 2** Manila falls as US forces retreat south towards Corregidor.
**January 17** Duncan briefs Arnold on the initial plan. Arnold selects Doolittle to organize, train, and equip aircrews for the Tokyo attack.
**January 23** First B-25B sent to Mid-Continent Airlines for modification.
**January 31** Target selection begins for the operation.
**February 1–2** Demonstration test of a B-25 bomber launch off the aircraft carrier *Hornet* succeeds.
**February 15** British forces surrender in Singapore.
**March** Japanese naval forces conduct operations in the Indian Ocean.
**March 1** 17th Bombardment Group volunteers arrive for training at Eglin Field, FL.
**March 16** Washington requests Stillwell to ask Chiang Kai-shek for permission to use airfields and to gather supplies and ground crews to support the raid.
**March 19** Nimitz is briefed on the raid; the decision is made to add another carrier to support the attack. Halsey is selected for the task.
**March 25** Doolittle and crews complete Eglin training.
**March 27** All aircraft and crew arrive at Sacramento Air Depot, CA for final aircraft checks.
**March 31** Doolittle and Halsey meet in San Francisco for final co-ordination.
**April 1** Aircraft and crew load on board the *Hornet* at Naval Air Station Alameda.
**April 2** TF-18 leaves San Francisco Bay for mission.
**April 8** TF-16 departs Pearl Harbor to rendezvous with TF-18.
**April 10** Japanese radio analysts claim to have received signals from TF-16.
**April 13** TF-16 and TF-18 rendezvous and move towards Japan.
**April 16** Chinese airfields are ready with fuel and support to receive the Doolittle raiders.
**April 17** *Hornet* and *Enterprise*, along with the cruisers, separate from TF-16. They speed towards their intended launch point.
**April 18,** *0310* Surface radar contact is made by *Enterprise* crew members with Japanese picket ships.
    *0508* *Enterprise* launches the first combat air patrols.
    *0522* Search planes are sent out; one crew believes they have seen a ship and that the Japanese have spotted them.

*0630* Nitto Maru reports to IJN Headquarters in Tokyo that it has seen three carriers. Coincidentally, Japanese launch routine patrol aircraft.

*0744* Hornet crew members, on watch, spot the Nitto Maru.

*0750* The USS Nashville attacks the Nitto Maru and eventually sinks her.

*0800* Halsey decides to launch the raid early since he believes TF-16 is now known to the Japanese.

*0803* Hornet increases speed and turns into the wind for launch.

*0820* Doolittle's plane is the first off the Hornet to bomb Tokyo.

*0921* The last B-25B leaves the Hornet. TF-16 immediately plots course for return to Pearl Harbor.

*1130* Japanese patrol aircraft are launched in search of TF-16.

*1200* Japanese observers spot bombers flying over Mito, and report their findings.

*1230* Doolittle attacks his first target in the Tokyo area.

*1245* The IJN's 26th Air Flotilla is ordered to search and destroy any attacking bombers.

*1424* USS Nashville sinks a patrol boat. Enterprise aircraft sink another.

*1445* First news of Tokyo bombing raid is broadcast via radio transmission.

**April 19** Doolittle promoted to the rank of Brigadier General.

**April 21** Roosevelt admits publicly the raid took place, claiming the planes were launched from their secret base at "Shangri-La."

**April 22** Doolittle crew members are all awarded the Distinguished Flying Cross.

**April 25** TF-16 returns safely to Pearl Harbor, with no damage or losses to ships.

**April 29** A few Doolittle crew members arrive in Chungking.

**May 3** Doolittle arrives in Chungking.

**May 5** Yamamoto's plan to attack Midway Island and draw the American Pacific Fleet into a decisive battle is approved.

**June 4–7** The Battle of Midway ends in a decisive American victory. IJN carrier supremacy is over.

**August 28** The Japanese try the two captured B-25 crews for war crimes.

**October 15** Hallmark, Farrow, and Spatz are executed by the Japanese. Others are sentenced to life imprisonment.

# 1943

**May 27** York and his crew escape into Iran.

**The American people were angry after Pearl Harbor and sought revenge. President Roosevelt looked for a way to satisfy them. The Doolittle Raid would serve this purpose. (National Archives)**

# OPPOSING COMMANDERS

President Franklin D. Roosevelt demanded that the United States strike back immediately at Japan. Here Roosevelt signs the Declaration of War against Japan on December 8, 1941. (National Archives)

Admiral Ernest J. King, CominCh and CNO, was a driving force behind the Navy and AAF raid on Japan. King pushed the concept of using carrier-launched, land-based bombers for the attack. (US Navy)

**B**y its very nature, the Doolittle Raid engaged relatively few combatants, and although the damage inflicted was comparatively minor it achieved a great strategic outcome. The planning and execution of the raid involved all levels from the US president down to a relatively low-ranking Army Air Forces (AAF) lieutenant colonel. Conversely, the Japanese planning for the homeland defense involved several commanders, split between sea (including naval air) and land-based air defenses. The nation also relied on available Imperial Japanese Navy (IJN) forces to counter any threat approaching the home islands.

## US COMMANDERS

The Doolittle Raid received the government's attention, politically and militarily, in its conception, planning, and operation. President Roosevelt championed the concept and motivation for the raid. Roosevelt had never served in uniform, but was no stranger to the military, having served as Assistant Secretary of the Navy. As president, Roosevelt initiated a program of prewar mobilization that included reinstatement of the draft, Army and Navy expansion, and America's rapid transformation into the "Arsenal of Democracy." Roosevelt was willing to take risks and often questioned established policies and laws. He involved himself heavily in military planning and operations more suited to lower levels of command.

Roosevelt's desire to strike back at Japan immediately after Pearl Harbor echoed throughout the government. The Commander-in-Chief US Fleet (CominCh) and the Chief of Naval Operations (CNO) Admiral Ernest J. King, and Lieutenant General Henry "Hap" Arnold, Chief of the AAF, heard his demands. King, a noted Anglophobe, was not a congenial commander. King graduated from the Naval Academy in 1901 and rapidly advanced through the ranks serving in surface warfare, submarines, and aviation. He earned his wings in May 1927 and later led the Bureau of Aeronautics. By 1941, King was a full admiral and was appointed commander of the Atlantic Fleet. After Pearl Harbor, Roosevelt appointed King to the unusual roles of CominCh and CNO. He was responsible for development and implementation of naval strategy for all theaters of operation.

Captain Francis S. Low, a CNO staff operations officer, became a key planner. Low, a submariner, had heard during a planning conference about using aircraft carriers to transport land-based planes to North Africa. The aircraft would fly off the carrier once they were in range of a friendly airfield. Low thought American forces could exploit this idea, but instead of delivering aircraft they would be used to attack targets in

Japan. Low was tasked with checking the readiness and availability of carriers. Another member of King's staff, air operations officer Capt Donald B. Duncan was assigned to support the effort. He would organize the air plan of attack.

The Navy commanders responsible for conducting the strategic attack revolved around the Pacific Fleet. Admiral Chester W. Nimitz, Commander-in-Chief Pacific Fleet (CINCPAC), was responsible for naval operations around Japan. Nimitz was in charge of operations in the Central Pacific. He shared his command with Gen Douglas MacArthur, who oversaw Southwest Pacific operations. Nimitz completed the US Naval Academy and was commissioned as an ensign in 1907. His career spanned surface and submarine assignments culminating in his promotion to full admiral in 1938. Nimitz became CINCPAC shortly after the Pearl Harbor attack.

Command of the task force carrying the Army bombers for the raid initially belonged to CAPT Marc A. Mitscher. Mitscher was the commanding officer of the newly commissioned USS *Hornet* that would carry the B-25s to Japan. In his early career, he served in armored cruisers, gunboats, and destroyers. He later trained as a naval aviator and was awarded his wings in June 1916. A Naval Academy graduate, Mitscher served in a variety of aviation assignments from executive officer on the aircraft carrier *Saratoga*, to command of the seaplane tender *Wright*, and served two years as Assistant Chief of the Bureau of Aeronautics.

The other operational naval commander was Admiral William F. "Bull" Halsey. Halsey would command a support task force for the raid from Pearl Harbor and later take command of all forces. Halsey also finished the Naval Academy and served in the antisubmarine forces during World War I aboard destroyers. He held assignments in Naval Intelligence and in October 1922 was ordered to serve a tour as a naval attaché in Berlin. Halsey was intrigued by carrier aviation and became an aviator in May 1935 when he was 52 years old. He later commanded the aircraft carrier USS *Saratoga*. In 1940, Halsey was elevated to the rank of vice admiral as the Commander Pacific Aircraft Battle Force.

General "Hap" Arnold, a 1903 graduate of the US Military Academy, first served in the infantry, but later became an aviator under the tutelage of the Wright brothers in June 1911. Arnold, as the first qualified Army pilot, was designated US Army Aviator Number 1. His career progressed steadily, and during World War I he was the youngest colonel in the Army. However, he never served in combat. He excelled in command and staff positions and headed the Army Air Corps in 1938 as a major general. Arnold became Chief of the AAF on June 30, 1941.

Lieutenant General Joseph "Vinegar Joe" Stillwell, a 1904 West Point graduate, commanded the China, Burma, and India (CBI) Theater for the United States. Stillwell would negotiate landing site support for the Doolittle raid from Generalissimo Chiang Kai-shek, head of the Nationalist Chinese movement. He was a tough officer who was awarded the Distinguished Service Medal for helping plan the St Mihiel offensive in 1918. He later served for almost 20 years in China, as a military attaché, observer, and commander. Chiang Kai-shek received his formal military education from the Paoting Military Academy and graduated in 1904. Chiang unified China in 1928, but was challenged by Mao

The Doolittle Raid was conducted in Admiral Chester W. Nimitz's area of responsibility, the Central Pacific. As CINCPAC, TF-16 fell under his command and control. (US Navy)

Vice Admiral William F. "Bull" Halsey took command of TF-16, composed of the *Hornet* and *Enterprise*, during the raid. Halsey ordered the attack earlier than planned after the task force was sighted by the Japanese. (US Navy)

General Henry "Hap" Arnold, AAF Chief, selected Doolittle, and was instrumental in the raid's planning. Arnold was a key player in providing the crews and aircraft for the attack. (US Air Force)

General Joseph Stillwell (right) had to persuade Generalissimo Chiang Kai-shek (left) to allow American bombers to land in China. Chiang was concerned about Japanese retribution, and his fears would later become reality. (National Archives)

Zedong's communists. He later claimed victory over them in 1934, but later could not contain the Japanese invasion of Manchuria in 1937.

Arnold selected Lieutenant Colonel James H. Doolittle, a member of his personal staff, to train, organize, and equip the Army bomber force. Doolittle was born in Alameda, CA on December 14, 1896. His family lived in a variety of areas, including Nome, AK where his father was a gold prospector. Doolittle attended the University of California, Berkeley, but left to enter the Army during World War I. He later graduated in 1922 with an engineering degree. Doolittle earned his wings on March 11, 1918, but never served in Europe.

"Jimmy" Doolittle was well known to a public enthralled with aviation before World War II. Doolittle continued as an Army aviator and test pilot after World War I. He taught himself aerobatics and helped persuade the public and a skeptical Congress of military aviation's value. He was a part of Brigadier General Billy Mitchell's First Provisional Air Brigade, which demonstrated aircraft could sink battleships in 1921. Doolittle achieved several "firsts" such as perfecting the outside loop, setting a world speed record, and flying across America in less than 24 hours in 1922. He also won the 1925 Schneider Marine Trophy. The Army awarded him the Distinguished Flying Cross for his cross-country flying trip.

Doolittle had achieved more accomplishments, in less time, than his contemporaries or his superiors. By 1925, he earned one of the first doctorates in aeronautical engineering from the Massachusetts Institute of Technology. Doolittle advanced as a test pilot for the Army at McCook Field in Dayton, Ohio and for the Navy at Mitchell Field in New York. His ultimate accomplishment was the development of instrument flying that allowed pilots to "fly blind." Doolittle personally tested take-off, flying, and landing by instruments in a fabric-covered cockpit on

CAPT Marc Mitscher (left) and LTC Jimmy Doolittle (right) ensured Doolittle's B-25B aircraft were combat ready. Mitscher guided TF-18 from Norfolk to its rendezvous with Halsey, while Doolittle led the attack. (US Navy)

September 24, 1929. This triumph allowed all-weather and night flying, which greatly expanded military and commercial aviation.

Doolittle's feats were not lost on others. Although he was allowed to seek opportunities to conduct aviation research, development, and testing, Doolittle was constrained within the military. The Shell Oil Company sought a way to enhance its aviation market and offered to triple Doolittle's major's salary and give him added flexibility for aviation experimentation. Doolittle resigned his active Air Corps commission, but retained a reserve one. He would continue to support test flights as a reservist. Under Shell employment, Doolittle was instrumental in pressing forward the development of 100-octane aviation fuel which powered aviation propulsion development to new heights. Despite his heavy schedule, Doolittle was still highly engaged in aviation racing. He won major speed racing competitions by flying a Laird Super Stallion in 1931 that resulted in the award of the Bendix Trophy and the 1932 Thompson Trophy in the Gee Bee R-1. The Gee Bee was infamous as a "death trap" and Doolittle later admitted that he was happy to walk away safely from it.

As the clouds of war gathered, Doolittle's career at Shell Oil was interrupted. He was recalled to active duty in 1940 as the United States mobilized. Arnold used him as a technical troubleshooter. One of his first duties was to ensure automobile manufacturers could switch to assembling Army aircraft. After the Pearl Harbor attack, Doolittle immediately requested a return to flight status. Instead, he was assigned to AAF Headquarters in Washington, working on special projects directly for Arnold.

## JAPANESE COMMANDERS

General Tojo Hideki led the government of Japan throughout most of World War II. He was also responsible for the defense of the nation, including Tokyo. (Military History Institute)

General Tojo Hideki, Prime Minister of Japan, oversaw the overall running of the country and its military organization. His government encouraged

16

Admiral Yamamoto Isoroku and the IJN were embarrassed at the Doolittle Raid's success. They felt they had failed to protect the emperor. This would lead to the Midway campaign. (National Archives).

Japanese expansion into the Pacific and Asia, although forces were allocated to defending the Japanese home islands, the emperor, and vital military, industrial, and political targets. The responsibility of Japan's home-island defense fell primarily upon IJN shoulders. Admiral Yamamoto Isoroku had kept Allied forces on the defensive by conducting a series of offensive actions, effectively reducing the possibility of a direct attack on Japan and securing peace. Yamamoto, a graduate of the Imperial Japanese Naval Academy in 1902, had witnessed the IJN's rise to prominence. He was a veteran of the critical battle of Tsushima in 1905; studied at Harvard University from 1919–21; traveled extensively in Europe and the United States as an admiral's aide; served as naval attaché in Washington; and commanded the aircraft carrier *Akagi* – all before 1930. His meteoric career path continued when he headed the Japanese contingent to the 1934 London Naval Conference that shaped IJN force structure. He later led efforts to abrogate the treaty. Yamamoto became Navy Minister from 1936–39, and forged the doctrine that the aircraft carrier was the IJN's principal offensive weapon. He rose to lead the Combined Fleet in 1940. The Doolittle Raid would both shake the confidence in Yamamoto's ability to defend Japan and shape his future thoughts on conducting an attack to defeat the US Pacific Fleet at Midway, the decisive conflict in the theater.

Rear Admiral Yamagata Massato controlled the 26th Air Flotilla that patrolled Japanese waters and offered naval air interception capability. He was born in 1891 and graduated from the IJN's Naval Academy. He initially served on the cruiser *Aso*, a prize from the Russo-Japanese War, and later progressed through several surface and shore commands. In 1934 he commanded the aircraft carrier *Hosho*. Yamagata became commander of the 26th Air Flotilla on April 1, 1942.

The 5th or Northern Fleet was the main naval force that protected the homeland and Tokyo. It was commanded by Vice Admiral Hosogaya Boshiro. Hosogaya graduated from the IJN's Naval Academy in 1908. He commanded at different levels throughout his early career. Notably, Hosogaya took command of the battleship *Mutsu* in 1934; was in charge of the Communications and later the Torpedo School; became vice admiral and was in charge of Port Arthur naval base; and was commander of the Central China Fleet from 1940 to 1941.

General Prince Higashikuni Naruhiko took charge of the Army units assigned to homeland defense. Higashikuni was related to Japan's Emperor Hirohito, but chose an army career. A 1908 Imperial Military Academy graduate, he gained success as head of the 5th Infantry Brigade, the 4th Army Division, the Military Aviation Department, and culminated his prewar career as the commander of the 2nd Army in China from 1938 to 1939. General Prince Higashikuni was a member of the Supreme War Council and by 1941 commanded the Army's General Defense Command (GDC), in charge of homeland defense interceptors, antiaircraft artillery, and air-raid warning.

# OPPOSING FORCES

## AMERICAN FORCES

American military forces involved in the Doolittle Raid comprised naval assets that delivered the strike elements and the AAF aircraft and crews making the attack. The naval units included two separate task forces that eventually merged into a single one. The initial naval forces were centered on the newly commissioned aircraft carrier *Hornet* (CV-8). The *Hornet* was launched on December 14, 1940 and was commissioned on October 20, 1941. At over 20,000 tons displacement and with a top speed of 34 knots per hour, the *Hornet* was the last and largest of the Yorktown carrier class. She was designed to carry about 72 aircraft. Commanded by Mitscher, the *Hornet* carried Air Group Eight aircraft. The group's Fighting Squadron Eight (VF-8) had 30 folding-wing Grumman F4F-4 Wildcats aboard during the raid. VF-8 pilots had exclusively used the older F4F-3s, but now received new F4F-4s in San Diego as their ship made its way to pick up the Doolittle Raiders from Naval Air Station Alameda on the San Francisco Bay. VF-8 pilots trained on two North American SNJ-3 single-engine aircraft used for instrument proficiency. This air group also had dive-bombing (VB-8), scouting (VS-8), and torpedo (VT-8) squadrons. VB-8 and VS-8 operated 24 Douglas SBD-3 Dauntless dive-bombers between them. VT-8 crews were assigned ten TBD-1 Devastator torpedo bombers. Mitscher's *Hornet* comprised the nucleus of Task Force 18 (TF-18) composed of Atlantic Fleet resources.

TF-18 elements included the *Vincennes* (CA 44), an Astoria class cruiser commissioned May 21, 1936, and the light cruiser *Nashville* (CL 43) from the Brooklyn class that entered service on October 2, 1937. The *Vincennes* displaced over 9,400 tons and could almost keep up with the *Hornet* at a maximum speed of 32.7 knots per hour. Her nine eight-

The raid used the carriers *Hornet* and *Enterprise*. *Enterprise* (CV-6) would provide air cover for the task force. The destroyer *Fanning* (DD 385), shown here in the foreground, provided screening and antisubmarine support. (US Navy)

The strike task force used four cruisers, including the USS *Northampton*. These ships required enormous amounts of fuel. Here the *Northampton* is refueled by the fleet oiler *Cimarron*. (US Navy)

The combined task force had eight destroyers on escort duty. CDR William R. Cooke, Jr. commanded the *Fanning* (DD 385) during the campaign. (US Navy)

inch guns provided the projection power to engage surface predators. The *Nashville*, was slightly heavier at 9,475 tons and was as fast as the *Hornet*. However, it carried smaller caliber main armament, 15 six-inch guns. TF-18 also contained Destroyer Division (Desdiv) 22 consisting of the Benson-Livermore class *Gwin* (DD 433), *Meredith* (DD 434), *Grayson* (DD 435), and *Monssen* (DD 436). It provided additional escort services and protection from submarine and aircraft threats. These destroyers mounted four single five-inch guns, two twin 40mm guns, two single 20mm weapons, and carried two quintuple 21-inch torpedo tubes. These ships entered service in 1940 and were the fastest ships in TF-18 with a maximum speed of 37 knots per hour. The last crucial TF-18 member was the *Cimarron* (AO 22), a fleet oiler that was commissioned on January 7, 1939. The *Cimarron* allowed for continuous operations once TF-18's elements had begun their journey towards Japan.

Although the *Hornet* maintained its full complement of aircraft, it needed air assets to maintain a combat air patrol to protect it from any enemy planes, scout for Japanese surface craft, or attack any threat. The *Hornet*'s naval aircraft could take-off, but could not recover them, since the B-25s were parked on its deck. Nimitz directed Halsey's TF-16, from Pearl Harbor, to rendezvous with TF-18 as it headed east towards Japan. TF-16's purpose was to provide air support and additional surface support for the *Hornet* once it reached enemy territory.

Halsey's TF-16 mirrored that of Mitscher's force. The flagship was the aircraft carrier USS *Enterprise* (CV 6), another Yorktown class vessel, with

Oilers were vital to the task force's success. Vessels such as the *Sabine* allowed the force to move across the Pacific. Note the rough sea conditions that plagued the voyage to Japan. (US Navy)

The *Enterprise* (CV 6) had a mix of aircraft. They included the three-man torpedo bomber, TBD-1 Devastators and the fixed-wing F-4F-3 Wildcat fighters. (US Navy)

its full complement of aircraft. *Enterprise* was five years older than the *Hornet*, but displaced over 100 tons less. The *Enterprise* had been designed and built under the 1922 Washington Naval Treaty and the 1930 London Conference that had reduced total tonnage on ships between its signatories. Japan, a signatory, would abrogate both treaties. The United States Congress, seeing potential war clouds over the horizon, authorized a naval construction boom under the Naval Expansion Act of May 17, 1938. The act allowed the Navy Department to build carriers that exceeded the carrier tonnage under the previous treaties. One result was an improved *Yorktown* class, the *Hornet*, but its changes were not significant enough to create a new aircraft carrier class.

The *Enterprise* had four aircraft squadrons under Air Group Six. *Enterprise*'s Fighting Squadron Six (VF-6) fielded 22 F4F-4s and five F4F-3s. The air group's dive-bombing squadron, VB-6, had a combination of 18 SBD-2 and three Dauntless aircraft. Additionally, the *Enterprise*'s scouting squadron, VS-6, was replaced with the aircraft carrier *Saratoga*'s VB-3 that also carried 18 SBD-2 and SBD-3 planes. CINCPAC transferred VB-3 in

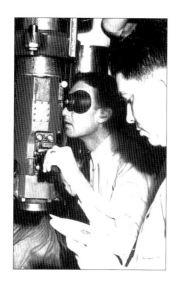

The Navy sent the submarines *Trout* and *Thresher* to gather weather and intelligence data. The crews would use the submarine's periscope to scout for TF-16. (National Archives)

place of VS-6 due to the scouting squadron's training status at Pearl Harbor. The last complement of aircraft came from the torpedo-bomber squadron, VT-6, that contained 18 TBD-1 Devastators. These aircraft would provide the combined task forces' naval air capability during the approach to Japan and their return to Pearl Harbor.

TF-16 also mirrored TF-18 in terms of escort and support ships. Cruiser support came from two elderly veterans, the *Salt Lake City* (CA 25) and the *Northampton* (CA 26). The *Salt Lake City*, a Pensacola class ship, was the smallest cruiser in the raid. However, she had a combination of two- and three-gun, eight-inch-caliber gun mounts, which gave her a total of ten guns, making her the most heavily armed of the surface ships. Commissioned on January 23, 1929, the *Salt Lake City* had a similar speed to the *Vincennes* and the *Northampton*. The *Northampton*, the lead ship and namesake of its heavy cruiser class, had one less eight-inch gun than the *Salt Lake City*. It also became a member of the fleet in 1929.

TF-16 also had destroyer escorts composed of Desdiv 12. The division was made up of the *Balch* (DD 363), *Benham* (DD 397), *Ellet* (DD 398), and *Fanning* (DD385). The Porter class *Balch* entered service in 1936 and was the largest of the TF-16 destroyers. It displaced about 1,805 tons and its crews manned eight five-inch guns and eight 21-inch torpedoes. The *Benham*, a Mahan class ship, was smaller at 1,450 tons. It had five five-inch guns, but compensated with twelve 21-inch torpedoes. She also was commissioned in 1936. The last two destroyers, *Ellet* and *Fanning*, were Craven class ships. This class continued the trend of fewer main five-inch guns, featuring only four weapons, but operated more torpedoes (16). These ships became part of the fleet in 1938. TF-16 also contained a fleet oiler, *Sabine*, to fuel operations.

When the two task forces combined, Halsey took command and they became TF-16. The destroyers, cruisers, and oilers were reorganized into functional groups. The task force was also supported independently by two submarines. The *Thresher* (SS 200) and the *Trout* (SS 202) were ordered to patrol the coastal waters off Japan to gather weather information during the raid's planning phase. Later, on April 10, both submarines were

The *Trout,* here in Pearl Harbor just before the Doolittle Raid, provided invaluable service to the success of the raid. Future submarine missions in the Pacific would strangle the Japanese economy and cripple her war industries. (US Navy)

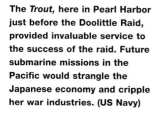

ordered to leave the Midway Island area and patrol around the area where TF-16 would launch the attack. Their orders were also to sink any enemy vessels in the area.

The main offensive punch from TF-16 would be delivered by the land-based Army bombers. The AAF B-25Bs came from the 17th Bombardment Group (BG) Medium that consisted of the 34th, 37th, and the 94th Bomb Squadrons. The 89th Reconnaissance Squadron was also part of the group. The 17th BG was the first operational AAF unit to receive the North American B-25 Mitchell bomber while it was stationed at McChord Field, WA in April 1941. The group began to transfer to Pendleton Field, OR on June 29, 1941 where it conducted antisubmarine patrols. One B-25 from the 17th BG sank the first Japanese submarine off the West Coast on December 24, 1941. They were later moved to Lexington County Airport near Columbia, SC where volunteers were sought for Special Aviation Project #1, the Doolittle Raid, and the remainder of the group supported antisubmarine actions against U-boats conducting Operation *Paukenschlag* (Drumbeat) around the Atlantic Ocean and Gulf of Mexico.

The B-25B was powered by twin-radial (air-cooled) Wright R-2600-9 Double Cyclone engines that could each deliver 1,700 horsepower at take-off. The aircraft had a crew of five: pilot, co-pilot, navigator-bombardier, engineer-gunner, and radio-gunner. The standard aircraft had top and ventral power turrets containing two .50-caliber machine guns and a nose-mounted .30-caliber machine gun. The plane could deliver 2,400 pounds

## Task Force 16
### Vice Admiral William F. Halsey, Jr.

**CAPT George D. Murray**
*Enterprise*
VB-6 , VF-6, VT-6, VB-3

**Rear Admiral Raymond A. Spruance**
*Northampton*  CAPT William D. Chandler
*Salt Lake City*  CAPT Ellis M. Zacharias
*Vincennes*  CAPT Frederick L. Riefkohl
*Nashville*  CAPT Francis S. Craven

**CAPT Marc A. Mitscher**
*Hornet*
VF-8, VB-8, VS-8, VT-8

**LTC James H. Doolittle**
16 B-25Bs

**CAPT Richard L. Conolly, Commander, Destroyer Squadron 6**

**CAPT Edward P. Sauer, Desdiv 12**
*Balch*  LCDR Harold H. Tiemroth
*Benham*  LCDR Joseph M. Worthington
*Ellet*  LCDR Francis H. Gardner
*Fanning*  CDR William R. Cooke, Jr.

**CDR Harold Holcomb, Desdiv 22**
*Grayson*  CDR Thomas M. Stokes
*Gwin*  CDR John M. Higgins
*Meredith*  LCDR Harry E. Hubbard
*Monssen*  CDR Roland M. Smoot

**CDR Houston L. Maples**
*Sabine*  CDR Houston L. Maples
*Cimarron*  CDR Russell M. Ihrig

of ordnance up to 2,000 miles. Crews flew at a maximum speed of 300 miles per hour at an altitude of 15,000 feet. Doolittle had to modify factory-fresh B-25Bs to extend the range of these aircraft.

# DOOLITTLE RAID CREWS

**After some analysis, the B-25B medium bomber was chosen as the aircraft to conduct the Doolittle Raid. The twin-engine aircraft would deliver a 2,000-pound bomb load on Japan. (US Navy)**

| Plane (number) | Pilot | Co-pilot | Navigator | Bombardier | Flight engineer/gunner |
|---|---|---|---|---|---|
| 1 (40-2344) | LTC James H. Doolittle | 2Lt Richard E. Cole | 2Lt Henry A. Potter | S/Sgt Fred A. Braemer | S/Sgt Paul J. Leonard |
| 2 (40-2292) | 1Lt Travis Hoover | 2Lt William N. Fitzhugh | 2Lt Carl R. Wildner | 2Lt Richard E. Miller | Sgt Douglas V. Radney |
| 3 (40-2270, "Whiskey Pete") | 1Lt Robert M. Gray | 2Lt Jacob E. Manch | 2Lt Charles J. Ozuk, Jr. | Sgt Aden E. Jones | Cpl Leland D. Faktor |
| 4 (40-2282) | 1Lt Everett W. Holstrom | 2Lt Lucian N. Youngblood | 2Lt Harry C. McCool | Sgt Robert J. Stephens | Cpl Bert M. Jordan |
| 5 (40-2283) | Capt David M. Jones | 2Lt Ross R. Wilder | 2Lt Eugene F. McGurl | 2Lt Denver V. Truelove | Sgt Joseph W. Manske |
| 6 (40-2298, "Green Hornet") | 1Lt Dean E. Hallmark | 2Lt Robert J. Meder | 2Lt Chase J. Nielsen | Sgt William J. Dieter | Sgt Donald E. Fitzmaurice |
| 7 (40-2261, "Ruptured Duck") | 1Lt Ted W. Lawson | 2Lt Dean Davenport | 2Lt Charles L. McClure | 2Lt Robert S. Clever | Sgt David J. Thatcher |
| 8 (40-2242) | Capt Edward J. York | 1Lt Robert G. Emmens | 2Lt Nolan A. Herndon | 2Lt Nolan A. Herndon | Flight Eng: S/Sgt Theodore H. Laban<br>Gunner: Sgt David W. Pohl |
| 9 (40-2303, "Whirling Dervish") | 1Lt Harold F. Watson | 2Lt James N. Parker, Jr. | 2Lt Thomas C. Griffen | Sgt Wayne M. Bissell | T/Sgt Eldred V. Scott |
| 10 (40-2250) | 1Lt Richard O. Joyce | 2Lt J. Royden Stork | 2Lt Horace E. Crouch | 2Lt Horace E. Crouch | Flight Eng: Sgt George E. Larkin, Jr.<br>Gunner: S/Sgt Edwin W. Horton, Jr |
| 11 (40-2249, "Hari Kari-er") | Capt C. Ross Greening | 2Lt Kenneth E. Reddy | 2Lt Frank A. Kappeler | S/Sgt William L. Birch | Sgt Melvin J. Gardner |
| 12 (40-2278, "Fickle Finger") | 1Lt William M. Bower | 2Lt Thadd H. Blanton | 2Lt William R. Pound, Jr. | T/Sgt Waldo J. Bither | S/Sgt Omer A. Duquette |
| 13 (40-2247) | 1Lt Edgar E. McElroy | 2Lt Richard A. Knobloch | 2Lt Clayton J. Campbell | M/Sgt Robert C. Bourgeois | Sgt Adam R. Williams |
| 14 (40-2297) | Maj John A. Hilger | 2Lt Jack A. Sims | 2Lt James H. Macia, Jr. | 2Lt James H. Macia, Jr. | Flight Eng: S/Sgt Jacob Eierman<br>Gunner: S/Sgt Edwin V. Bain |
| 15 (40-2267) | 1Lt Donald G. Smith | 2Lt Griffin P. Williams | 2Lt Howard A. Sessler | 2Lt Howard A. Sessler | Flight Eng: Sgt Edward J. Saylor<br>Flight Surgeon: 1Lt Thomas A. White, Medical Corps |
| 16 (40-2268, "Bat Out of Hell") | 1Lt William G. Farrow | 2Lt Robert L. Hite | 2Lt George Barr | Cpl Jacob D. DeShazer | Sgt Harold A. Spatz |

# JAPANESE FORCES

Home island Japanese defenses were undertaken by a mixture of IJN, Army, and Japanese Army Air Force (JAAF) units. The IJN was given the primary responsibility for protecting the emperor and Japan from an attack. Although the Army did have anti-aircraft artillery (AAA) batteries and the JAAF maintained a force of obsolete interceptors around the country, the Army, like the IJN, devoted most of its resources to offensive operations instead of homeland defense. An air attack on Japan, just after the start of the war, was considered unlikely throughout the Japanese government. Tojo proclaimed on November 4, 1941:

> *I do not think the enemy could raid Japan proper from the air immediately after the outbreak of hostilities. Some time would elapse before the enemy could attempt such raids. I believe that enemy air attacks against Japan proper in the early stages of the war would be infrequent and would be carried out by carrier-based planes.*

The total homeland defense forces to counter enemy aircraft stood at 100 JAAF and 200 IJN interceptors. There were 500 Army AAA pieces and 200 Navy weapons. These forces, however, had to defend a vast swathe of territory.

IJN forces were composed of the Outer Combat Forces (OCF), the Combined Fleet and China Area Fleet, and the Inner Combat Forces (ICF). OCF, commanded by Yamamoto, conducted offensive operations. ICF, composed of naval districts, provided homeland defense, surface escort, and operational support to OCF. ICF responsibility included defending the area from the northern Kuril Islands south to Formosa, and Port Arthur west to the home islands. Responsibility for the Tokyo defenses fell to the Yokosuka Naval District. ICF attention

The 244th Air Regiment defended the Tokyo area with obsolete Ki-27 Nate fighters. The Ki-27s failed to shoot down any B-25Bs. The unexpected Doolittle Raid forced the Japanese to improve the homeland's air defenses. (National Archives)

focused on the submarine threat to Japan. Antisubmarine nets, mines, and some air groups were assigned the mission to protect harbor entrances. Additionally, obsolete AAA batteries were located at each naval base.

ICF assets also included the 5th or Northern Fleet, under Hosogaya, which provided a capability to search and defeat any enemy naval force capable of attacking Japan, including an aircraft-carrier strike, submarine torpedo attacks, or shelling. This fleet operated forces from 600 to 700 nautical miles east of Japan. About 50 picket ships were deployed offshore to detect any enemy fleet activities. These picket ships used visual identification and would broadcast their observations over Navy frequencies. The Army had to monitor the Navy circuit to gather any information or rely on Navy notification – a major communications concern.

By April 1941, the 5th Fleet had several assets available to defend Tokyo. These forces included the 21st Cruiser Division, a patrol flotilla, the 26th Air Flotilla, and support units. The 26th Air Flotilla was composed of land attack and carrier-based naval aircraft from shore installations and a detachment from the aircraft carrier *Kaga*. The carrier aircraft included the Mitsubishi A6M2 Zero (*Zero-sen* to the Japanese), the Aichi D3A Val dive-bomber, and the Nakajima B5N Kate. The single-engine Zero had distinguished itself as a formidable naval fighter in China, at Pearl Harbor, and in other early campaigns. The aircraft had two 7.7mm machine guns in its fuselage and contained a pair of 20mm, Type 99 cannon in its wings. The twin-seat Val used fixed landing gear and could carry only 816 pounds of conventional bombs for approximately 900 miles. Kate bombers generally carried torpedoes, but could also deliver conventional bombs. This aircraft was becoming obsolete due to its slow speed. The Northern Fleet also operated twin-engine Mitsubishi G4M Betty land-based search and attack bombers. The Betty had a cruising speed of 195 miles per hour at 13,125 feet and a maximum range of 2,694 miles.

The Army organized the GDC for homeland defense on July 12, 1941. GDC home island defenses were organized into geographical military districts. The Tokyo area fell under the Eastern District. The majority of JAAF units assigned to GDC were mostly training units. The 1st Air Army defended the Tokyo area with interceptors. The organization of this unit was convoluted since it was primarily under a training command. The Inspectorate General of Army Aviation had jurisdiction over its operational activities, but the Army Aeronautical Department controlled the distribution of planes and logistics. There was a decided lack of unified command.

The 244th Air Regiment, under the 1st Air Army, operated under the Kanto Air Defense Sector; it was responsible for Tokyo, Yokohama, and Kawasaki – all targets in the Doolittle Raid. The 244th had the highest priority to project the most vital area of Japan: the Imperial Palace, industrial Yokohama, and key military installations. The regiment was based at Chofu, southeast of Tokyo, and had 50 Nakajima Type 97 Ki-27 Nate aircraft, an obsolete plane. The JAAF also based some Kawasaki Ki-61 Hien, single-seat fighters, at Mito. Superficially, these aircraft appeared similar to the German Messerschmitt Bf 109. Additionally, there were several air training fields around Tokyo serving about 100

# JAPANESE AREAS OF DEFENSIVE RESPONSIBILITY, APRIL 1942

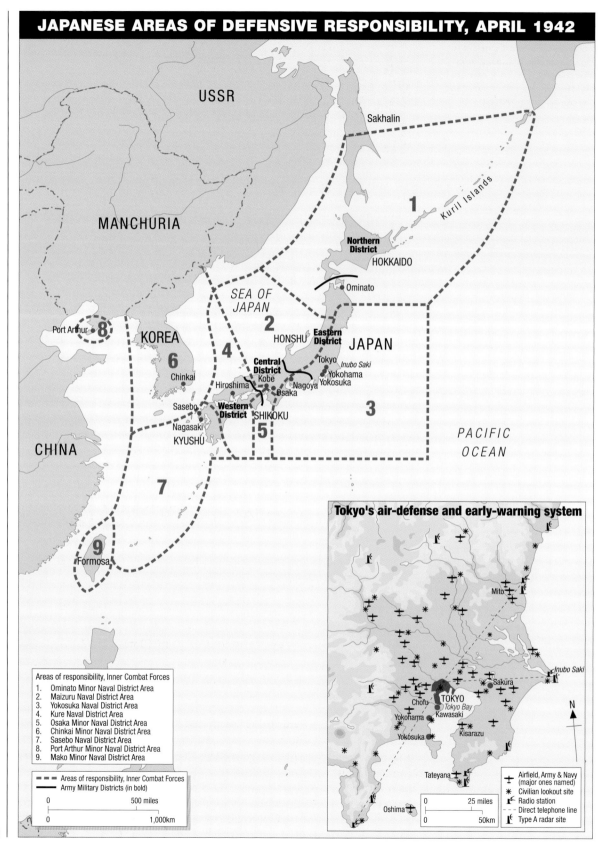

USSR

MANCHURIA

**1**

Kuril Islands

Sakhalin

**Northern District**

HOKKAIDO

Ominato

Port Arthur **8**

KOREA

SEA OF JAPAN

**2**

HONSHU

**Eastern District**

JAPAN

**6**

Chinkai

**4**

**Central District**

Kobe

Tokyo

Inubo Saki

Yokohama
Yokosuka

Hiroshima

Nagoya

Osaka

Sasebo

**Western District**

SHIKOKU

**3**

PACIFIC OCEAN

Nagasaki

KYUSHU

**5**

CHINA

**7**

**9**

Formosa

### Areas of responsibility, Inner Combat Forces

1. Ominato Minor Naval District Area
2. Maizuru Naval District Area
3. Yokosuka Naval District Area
4. Kure Naval District Area
5. Osaka Minor Naval District Area
6. Chinkai Minor Naval District Area
7. Sasebo Naval District Area
8. Port Arthur Minor Naval District Area
9. Mako Minor Naval District Area

- - - - Areas of responsibility, Inner Combat Forces
———— Army Military Districts (in bold)

| 0 | 500 miles |
| 0 | 1,000km |

## Tokyo's air-defense and early-warning system

Mito

Inubo Saki

Sakura

Chofu

TOKYO
Tokyo Bay

Yokohama

Kawasaki

Yokosuka

Kisarazu

Tateyama

Oshima

N

| 0 | 25 miles |
| 0 | 50km |

✈ Airfield, Army & Navy (major ones named)
✳ Civilian lookout site
⚲ Radio station
- - - Direct telephone line
⚲ Type A radar site

26

aircraft. The area around Nagoya had ten interceptors and the JAAF assigned 20 to the vicinity of Osaka–Kobe.

Fixed locations, primarily airfields and other important industrial and government locations, had AAA defenses. By April 1942 there were 150 AAA weapons defending Tokyo. The primary weapons were Model 88 (1928) 75mm pieces.

The Japanese Army also operated an air-raid warning system. These included military and civilian lookout posts. Although these posts normally had radio or telephone communications, there were several shortcomings. Many simply failed to recognize enemy aircraft, improperly identified friendly ones, or duplicated reports. The Army was also building a radar system that could detect objects, but only if they passed directly through its fixed beam. This radar, Type A, system was established along the coastline and served as perimeter warning. The Army and Navy also listened for Allied radio broadcasts to determine whether a naval task force or aircraft formation was near. Regardless of the source of warning, moving interceptors to the right location and altitude took time, more than an hour. A quick enemy strike could avoid a major interception effort.

| Table 1: air defense interception sequence | |
| --- | --- |
| **Action** | **Elapsed time** |
| Hostile aircraft detected at 200–250km<br>Hostile planes' existence confirmed<br>Air defense units alerted | 3 minutes |
| Report reaches headquarters and interceptors ordered to take-off | 7 minutes |
| Lead planes of air regiment take-off | 15 minutes |
| All planes take alert stations and gain required altitude (10,000m) | 50–60 minutes |
| **Total** | **75–85 minutes** |

Japanese homeland defense command and control was fragmented. There was no centralized control of air defense activities; communications between the IJN, JAAF, and the Army were virtually non-existent. Resources were devoted increasingly to major offensive operations; homeland defense was an afterthought. The Japanese military command was overconfident that an attack would not come, and there was limited capability to detect and thwart an air attack. They lacked organization to conduct an effective defense against a carrier-based aircraft attack – something that Tojo had predicted as the most likely threat.

## Northern Fleet – 5th Fleet
### Vice Admiral Hosogaya Boshiro

**Headquarters Group**
21st Cruiser Division
*Tama* Light cruiser
*Kiso* Light cruiser
*Sagi* Destroyer
*Kaiho Maru* Gunboat
*Hakuho Maru* Minesweeper
*Kimikawa Maru* Seaplane tender

**Patrol Flotilla**
**Rear Admiral Horiuchi S.**
22nd Picket Boat Squadron
*Awata Maru* Transport
*Asaka Maru* Transport
1st Picket Boat Group
2nd Picket Boat Group
3rd Picket Boat Group

**26th Air Flotilla**
**Rear Admiral Yamagata Massato**
Kisarazu Air Group
Misawa Air Group
6th Air Group
Marcus Island Detachment
Kaoya Air Group
Detachment from 4th Air Group
Detachment from *Kaga*

**Bonin Island Task Force**
**Read Admiral Fujimori S.**

7th Base Force
ChiChi-Jima Air Group
10th Converted Gunboat Division
17th Converted Minesweeper Division
66th Converted Subchaser Division

**Support Unit**

*Shiriya* Fleet oiler
*Nissan Maru* Fleet oiler
*Akashisan Maru* Transport
*#22 Toko Maru* Transport

---

### COMPOSITION OF 6TH AIR ATTACK GROUP

**Rear Admiral Yamagata Massato**
**26th Air Flotilla**

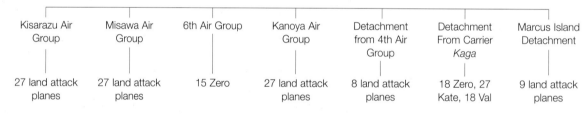

| Kisarazu Air Group | Misawa Air Group | 6th Air Group | Kanoya Air Group | Detachment from 4th Air Group | Detachment From Carrier *Kaga* | Marcus Island Detachment |
|---|---|---|---|---|---|---|
| 27 land attack planes | 27 land attack planes | 15 Zero | 27 land attack planes | 8 land attack planes | 18 Zero, 27 Kate, 18 Val | 9 land attack planes |

Note: *Land attack planes were probably G4M Mitsubishi Betty twin-engine bombers.*

---

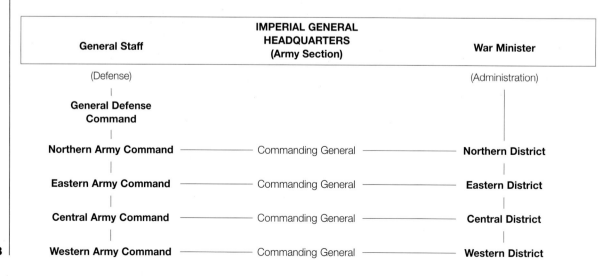

| | IMPERIAL GENERAL HEADQUARTERS (Army Section) | |
|---|---|---|
| **General Staff** | | **War Minister** |

(Defense)

**General Defense Command**

| **Northern Army Command** | Commanding General | **Northern District** |
| **Eastern Army Command** | Commanding General | **Eastern District** |
| **Central Army Command** | Commanding General | **Central District** |
| **Western Army Command** | Commanding General | **Western District** |

(Administration)

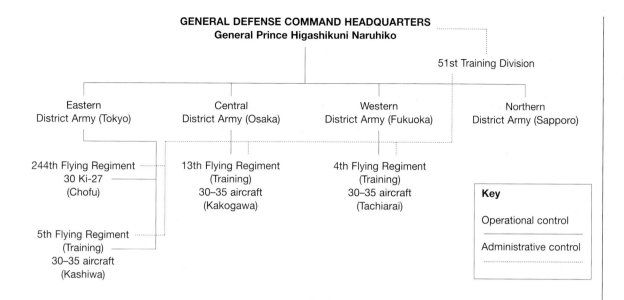

**GENERAL DEFENSE COMMAND HEADQUARTERS**
**General Prince Higashikuni Naruhiko**

51st Training Division

Eastern
District Army (Tokyo)

Central
District Army (Osaka)

Western
District Army (Fukuoka)

Northern
District Army (Sapporo)

244th Flying Regiment
30 Ki-27
(Chofu)

13th Flying Regiment
(Training)
30–35 aircraft
(Kakogawa)

4th Flying Regiment
(Training)
30–35 aircraft
(Tachiarai)

5th Flying Regiment
(Training)
30–35 aircraft
(Kashiwa)

| Key | |
|---|---|
| Operational control | |
| Administrative control | |

# PLANNING THE RAID

Through December 1941 and into early 1942, the strategic environment in the Pacific was desperate for the United States. The Pacific Fleet had been battered and American ground forces were in retreat in the Philippines. The IJN and Japanese Army were triumphant from Southeast Asia to the Central Pacific. America and her Allies could do little to stem the tide of Japanese conquests. Morale ebbed lower with each Japanese victory. Many in Washington feared that China might succumb to Japan.

Roosevelt needed to change the war's direction. Army planners wanted to attack the Japanese homeland two days after Pearl Harbor. Some planners believed "the best way to offset this initial defeat is to burn Tokyo and Osaka." Unfortunately, long-range bomber bases in the Philippines were gone; besides, there were few B-17s in the AAF inventory and those would be needed in Europe. Chinese airfields did not offer a viable solution. An air raid from Russia was possible, but the Soviet Union did not want to risk war with Japan. West Coast, Hawaiian, or Aleutian-based bomber flights were out of range. Despite this, Roosevelt was determined to "find ways and means of carrying home to Japan proper, in the form of a bombing raid, the real meaning of war." By January 1942, both King and Arnold were examining attack options.

Roosevelt pressed the military to conduct a bombing raid on Japan "as soon as humanly possible to bolster morale of America and her Allies." The only viable option seemed to involve a carrier-based aircraft

Loading and launching B-25B bombers on an aircraft carrier deck would take some effort. The Army and Navy had tested the concept, but had never used it during an operation. (US Navy)

Early in the war, US submarines attacked Japanese merchant ships and naval vessels throughout Japan's home waters. The two submarines supporting the Doolittle Raid could attack any ships that threatened TF-16 and send them to the bottom – a fate that awaits this sinking Japanese destroyer. (US Navy)

Navy F4F-3s could launch from the *Hornet* in an emergency, but they could not return. To provide adequate air cover, Nimitz ordered Halsey and the *Enterprise* to aid the attack. (US Navy)

strike. The Japanese had recently proven the concept in Hawaii, as had the Royal Navy at Taranto against the Italian fleet. However, carriers would need to approach close inshore to allow naval aircraft to hit Japan. This would risk the Pacific Fleet's remaining offensive capability, her aircraft carriers. The loss of any carrier might prove fatal to American capability.

An approach was studied to launch land-based B-25 bombers from a carrier's deck. This alternative would allow carriers to launch the planes further from the Japanese coastline, and they could land east of Japan. Arnold believed the plan originated from the Anglo-American Arcadia Conference held from December 22, 1941 to January 14, 1942. Arcadia served to co-ordinate Allied war objectives and strategy. One area examined was American support to a North African invasion. King had suggested using aircraft carriers to ferry aircraft to the area, where one carrier would carry 80–100 AAF fighters and another heavier bombers. The AAF aircraft could launch into action immediately from their carriers and land at Allied-controlled airfields. The concept seemed feasible, but heavier bombers and transports had never taken off from a carrier.

Low further developed the concept and Duncan expanded it to involve the newly commissioned *Hornet* as a transport for land-based bombers. Other carriers were engaged in operations and the *Hornet* was earmarked for the Pacific Fleet anyway. The AAF had several medium bombers capable of launching the attack: the B-18, B-23, B-25, and B-26. By 1942, the B-18 was obsolete. The B-23, an upgraded B-18, had too large a wingspan for carrier operations. The AAF's B-26 was untried, but

did have the range and payload. Unfortunately, it needed a longer take-off run than a carrier's deck. The only viable aircraft was the B-25. The AAF would have to reduce the aircraft's weight and add fuel capacity to increase its range.

One unanswered question was whether the bombers would return to the carriers upon mission completion or continue to China or Russia. Neither the B-25 nor other bombers had tailhooks to land on the carriers. The B-25 also had tricycle landing gear and it had a very high approach speed. A carrier landing was unfeasible. Another option included bombers returning near the carriers, where the planes would then ditch into the sea; this alternative was eliminated. Negotiations to land AAF B-25s in Russia dissolved quickly. The Russians feared that the Japanese would see the landings as a sign that they were aiding the American war effort against them. China was chosen as the destination. Five possible airfields were selected: Kweilin, Kian, Yushan, Chuchow, and Lishui (also called Chuchow). Lishui, was designated a primary landing site, lying 200 miles southeast of Shanghai and 70 miles inland. These sites would serve as refueling stops, allowing the crews to fly to Chungking. Lieutenant General Joseph Stillwell, commander of US Forces in China, had to obtain approval for the sites from Generalissimo Chiang Kai-shek. Neither Stillwell nor Chiang were notified initially of the raid's details. Chiang was concerned that any military co-operation with the Americans would lead to instant Japanese reprisals. Still, he agreed, under the strain of Stillwell's constant pressure. Following the landings, the planes would be assigned to the Chinese Air Force under the 10th Air Force.

Duncan's original plan was to launch bombers about 500 miles off Japan from the *Hornet*. The flight from Tokyo to the Chinese coast was at least 1,200 miles. Given the distances, combat operations, questionable weather, and the need for a safety margin, the B-25s would have to deliver the strike at 2,400 miles with an ordnance load of 2,000 pounds. The planes would conduct a low-altitude bombing raid on Tokyo and military and industrial targets in the surrounding areas, not civilian ones. Doolittle was adamant that the Imperial Palace be avoided, believing it to be a historic and religious site. Additionally, he feared that a direct attack on the emperor would galvanize Japanese morale, much as happened to the British during the Battle of Britain. Low-altitude flying would help the crews avoid detection, increase bomb accuracy, and reduce their vulnerability to AAA fire. The plan was later modified to launch the planes within 400 miles, and possibly at 650 miles.

There were three operational attack plans:

**Option 1.** Take-off three hours before dawn; arrive over target at first light. This would allow for maximum surprise and provide security to the carriers as well. However, a night launch for the AAF bombers might be difficult and deck lights would be necessary for the take-offs, thus illuminating the carriers.

**Option 2.** Take off at dawn, conduct attacks in daylight, and proceed to landing by dusk. This option created conditions for better navigation and bombing results. However, enemy AAA and interceptors would be more effective against the bombers in daylight.

**Option 3.** Take off just before dark, bomb at night, and arrive at the landing site at dawn. A plane, Doolittle's, would act as a pathfinder by dropping incendiaries over Tokyo to guide the rest of the bombers to the area. This option provided security for the task force and bomber force, but decreased the crew's ability to identify their targets. This was the preferred option since it maximized surprise and minimized risk.

If the carriers were spotted by an enemy force, then the bombers would be launched immediately. Duncan also reviewed weather patterns over Japan and considered April to be the best period for the operation. King approved the concept.

The initial plan was finalized and Duncan briefed Arnold on January 17. Arnold also concurred with the concept and selected Doolittle to

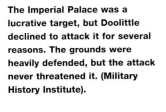

The Imperial Palace was a lucrative target, but Doolittle declined to attack it for several reasons. The grounds were heavily defended, but the attack never threatened it. (Military History Institute).

prepare the AAF bomber force and crew for the mission. On January 23, Doolittle sent one B-25 to Mid-Continent Airlines in Minneapolis, MN to add fuel tanks and remove unneeded equipment. Eventually, Mid-Continent modified 24 aircraft. The aircraft received new fuel bladders, bomb shackles, cameras, and the removal of the ventral gun turret. This turret had given crews problems due to hydraulic power failures. Since radio silence was vital, the 230-pound liaison radio set was removed. Crew members also replaced the sensitive high-altitude Norden bombsight, since the attacks would come at lower altitudes and the AAF did not want it to fall into enemy hands. Instead, a crew member designed a 20-cent bomb sight christened the "Mark Twain" to replace the $10,000 Norden sight.

The details of the highly classified plan were known only to Arnold, King, Duncan, and Doolittle. Arnold provided some basic concepts to Roosevelt on January 28. Roosevelt was made aware of the details only after the attack. By January 31, the AAF's Brigadier General Carl Spaatz had provided Doolittle with specific targets and maps from Arnold's Intelligence Staff.

The planners started to work on specific concerns such as the likelihood of a successful B-25B take-off from the *Hornet*. Test flights occurred on February 1 and 2 that proved the concept. Doolittle envisioned 15 B-25s would take part in the raid. Originally, 18 planes would have conducted the raid if they could return to the carriers. Each bomber would carry a combination of 500-pound M-43 demolition bombs and M-54 incendiary cluster bombs containing 128 four-pound bomblets each.

The planes and crews for the bomb mission all came from the 17th BG. Volunteers were culled from the group for 24 crews and ground personnel while the 17th BG was in South Carolina. After their selection, they arrived at Eglin Field, FL to undergo training. The last crews arrived at Eglin on March 1. Doolittle told the group that their mission was to bomb Japan. Doolittle had planned on using only 15 B-25s to conduct the raid, but needed spare crews to form a replacement pool. For this reason, and to maximize security, all the gathered crews would embark on the raid.

The crews had little time to relax in training. They had to learn how to take-off with a 31,000-pound B-25 from a carrier's deck, conduct low-altitude bombing, succeed at cross-country flying, perform night navigation, and practice gunnery. Bomb runs were made at 1,500 feet to avoid bomb fragmentation. The crews also had to adjust to the newly modified B-25Bs and test their capabilities. They had to gain maximum aircraft performance with minimum fuel consumption. They tried several approaches, including lowering speed, carburetor adjustments, and replacing the propellers, all of which helped.

The Navy was also busy planning for the raid. The *Hornet* would move from Norfolk, VA, via the Panama Canal, and load the planes and crews at Alameda. However, the *Hornet* alone would be vulnerable to an attack despite the presence of other ships in TF-18. After a March 19 briefing on the raid by Duncan, Nimitz decided to send another carrier task force, under Halsey, to support the effort and meet TF-18, as it headed west. The two carriers and the task force cruisers would speed to within launch range, allow the B-25s to begin their flight, and then make a high-speed return to Pearl Harbor.

Although not in the direct military chain of command, Emperor Hirohito was the leader of the Japanese Empire. His safety was the primary mission of Japanese defensive forces. (Military History Institute)

# THE DOOLITTLE RAID

## FINAL PREPARATIONS

The Doolittle group largely completed training in about a month. Doolittle was originally slated to be only a project leader for preparing the mission, which was entitled "Special Aviation Project #1." Doolittle convinced a doubting Arnold that he should command the raid on one of his many trips to Washington to inform Arnold of the training progress. He did not entrust reports to telephone communications for security concerns.

The bomber crews completed preparations for the raid and left for Alameda on March 25. From the original 24 aircraft, only 22 made the trip west. One bomber was destroyed as a result of a take-off accident; the other was damaged with a landing gear failure. Ground crews did not have sufficient time to repair the damaged aircraft.

The B-25B crews traveled to California from Phoenix, AZ via San Antonio, TX. From Phoenix, the group flew to March Field in southern California, and all aircraft had reached the Sacramento Air Depot by March 27. The B-25s were inspected and some equipment replaced, such as the propellers. Unfortunately, the Sacramento Air Depot technicians were unaware of the mission or the aircraft's special calibrations, such as the carburetor adjustments. They unknowingly realigned the carburetors to standard settings, meaning the pilots would be unable to attain their maximum aircraft performance. Fortunately, one of the aircrews noticed a standard carburetor with a different serial number installed on an engine. The adjustments and some new equipment had to be removed and returned to their previous settings.

The entire Doolittle group reached the shores of San Francisco Bay and Alameda on April 1. Doolittle and Halsey had earlier met to finalize

**The *Kaga* and other IJN ships were conducting operations throughout the Pacific at the time of the raid. America feared that, without a major turn of events, Japanese forces would become firmly entrenched in the Pacific. (National Archives)**

TF-18 left San Francisco Bay on April 2. Navy Blimp L-8 carries a crate of essential B-25B aircraft parts including navigator domes. (US Navy)

co-ordination on March 31. Nimitz and Halsey had some doubts about the raid. IJN forces were operating as far as the Indian Ocean, had bombed Ceylon, and would later sink Royal Navy ships such as the carrier HMS *Hermes*. The Navy was unaware of IJN intentions and needed to respond to any new threat. Sending carriers close to Japan was considered suicide to any ships, aircraft, and crews. King was also concerned, until CINCPAC's intelligence staff determined that the Japanese had terminated their major operations in the Indian Ocean; fears about an immediate attack on Australia lessened. Instead, the staff believed the Japanese would target New Guinea and conduct a Combined Fleet major operation in the Central Pacific area. Nimitz was being asked to deploy two out of his four Pacific Fleet carriers in enemy waters under his most experienced commander, Halsey. Despite the risks, Nimitz gave full support to the attack.

Mitscher ordered 16 of the B-25s loaded onto the *Hornet*'s deck; all but one would be launched against Tokyo. The AAF contingent numbered 70 officers and 130 enlisted members. Although Doolittle had trained all crews to take-off from the length of a carrier's deck, no one from the group had witnessed a B-25 launch from a carrier. The sixteenth aircraft would provide a demonstration 100 miles offshore and return to California. The extra plane did "fit," and still allowed crews the required 467 feet of carrier deck for take-off. The Navy's LT H.L. Miller, who had instructed the bomber crews at Eglin on carrier take-off procedures, would pilot the flight. However, concerns were voiced that spies would spot the planes on the *Hornet*'s deck, and that a demonstration flight would alert them to its intended mission.

## THE TASK FORCE SETS SAIL

TF-18 left San Francisco Bay at 1000 on April 2 in foggy conditions. Air patrol support, consisting of Navy Consolidated PBY Catalina seaplanes to defend the task force against submarine attack, was provided by the Western Sea Frontier until late that afternoon. The last direct contact made by the *Hornet* with the mainland was with Navy Blimp L-8, which had to deliver two boxes of navigator domes that were not installed at

OPPOSITE **Many of Doolittle's crews decorated their aircraft with nose art. Captain Ross Greening christened his plane "Hari Kari-er." (US Navy)**

TF-18 only had one delivery of supplies during its transit to meet TF-16. Navy blimp L-8 made a delivery off the coast of California. (US Navy)

Sacramento Air Depot. All future routine communications between TF-18 ships was completed by semaphore. Radio crews maintained strict silence, unless it was absolutely necessary to receive or transmit messages. Once well out to sea, the Doolittle mission's objective was released to the Navy crews. According to Mitscher, its release created an atmosphere where "morale reached a new high, there to remain until after the attack was launched."

Halsey's TF-16 left Pearl Harbor at 1232 on April 8. The *Enterprise* led the force south of Pearl Harbor, where she recovered her Air Group 8 aircraft. TF-16 proceeded on a northwesterly course where it would intersect with TF-18's course. Heavy seas and winds created problems for both task forces. Aircraft patrols were suspended. Mitscher had to reduce TF-16's speed to limit possible structural damage to the *Cimarron*. Despite heavy seas, the *Cimarron* did manage to refuel the destroyers on April 8. However, a refueling for the *Hornet*, planned for the next day, was canceled due to continuing bad weather conditions. The seas, winds, and rain for both task forces continued to limit their speed. TF-18 was ordered to delay its rendezvous with TF-16 until April 13.

The bomber crews were kept busy with additional training during the cruise. Navy LCDR Stephen Jurika provided lectures on Japan and the targets. Jurika had served in Tokyo from 1939 to 1941 as a naval attaché. He helped the crew to pinpoint targets by providing landmarks to navigate, such as rivers and bridges. He also gave the pilots information on AAA locations and fighter tactics. Gunnery and turret practice was maintained by crews by shooting at kites. Crews also maintained proficiency in celestial navigation for night flying. Navigators practiced sighting stars on deck and in their aircraft. They were supervised by the *Hornet*'s navigating officer. 1Lt T.A. White, AAF flight surgeon on the mission, instructed crews on field sanitation and first aid. The maintenance crews also checked the B-25s to maintain their readiness.

TF-16 had set a course of 310° from the Hawaiian Islands and was slowly converging on TF-18. The first contact between TF-16 and TF-18 was made at 1630 on April 12 through a radar contact from 230° about 130 miles away. The two task forces met at latitude 38° 00' North and longitude 180° 00' East at 0600 on April 13.

The two task forces became TF-16 under Halsey's command. Halsey ordered his command to take a course 265° heading east towards Japan at 16 knots. The attack was planned for April 19, having adjusted for the speed and weather conditions. The combined task

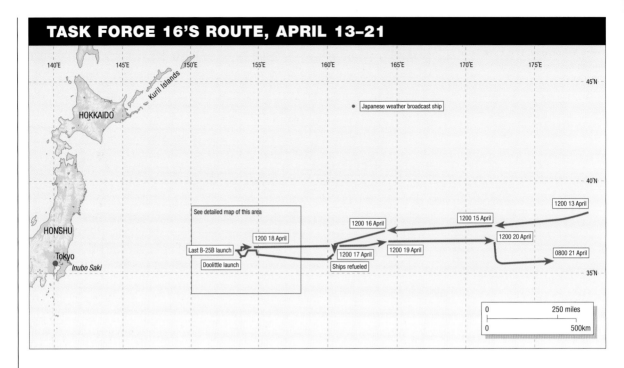

Japanese weather broadcast ship

See detailed map of this area

1200 13 April

1200 16 April

1200 15 April

1200 18 April

1200 20 April

Last B-25B launch

1200 17 April

1200 19 April

0800 21 April

Doolittle launch

Ships refueled

0    250 miles
0    500km

force had ample time to transit the Central Pacific. Still, security was maintained at a high level. Aircraft reconnaissance flights were flown from the *Enterprise* to search the waters 200 miles from the task force. Similarly, all ships maintained a close watch for enemy surface activities.

The submarines *Trout* and *Thresher* had begun patrols of the area where TF-16 would operate, close to Japanese home waters off Honshu. The *Trout* did fire two torpedoes against two small cargo ships on April 9, but they missed. On April 10, the submarine attacked another steamer, but also failed to score a success. Finally, on April 11, the crew fired two torpedoes at a large freighter, but only one torpedo hit the target and she survived. The *Thresher* was patrolling off Inubo Saki, where the B-25s would pass from the Pacific Ocean into Tokyo Bay, gathering weather information. Like the *Trout*, the *Thresher*'s crews attacked several targets, including a 10,000-ton freighter on April 10 that escaped destruction. However, she was more successful against a 5,000-ton freighter near Yokohama in Tokyo Bay. The *Thresher* sank the freighter in less than three minutes. The submarine was subsequently attacked by a Japanese sub-chaser and depth-charged. This attack damaged the submarine, but she continued to patrol Japanese waters and report weather information. The *Trout* and the *Thresher* reported the absence of any large naval force that could endanger TF-16.

The long cruise to Japan was highlighted by a simple "ceremony" using donated Japanese medals awarded to Navy crewmen during a 1908 port call to Tokyo. These medals represented the Japanese government's desire to show friendship towards and co-operation with the United States. Three ex-Navy veterans sent the medals to Washington in the hope that one day they would be used in some manner. Secretary of the Navy Frank Knox collected the medals and sent them to Nimitz. Nimitz provided the medals to Special Aviation Project #1. Doolittle and Mitscher decided to "return with interest" the medals by attaching them to ordnance destined to be

**The detailed map indicated above appears on page 50.**

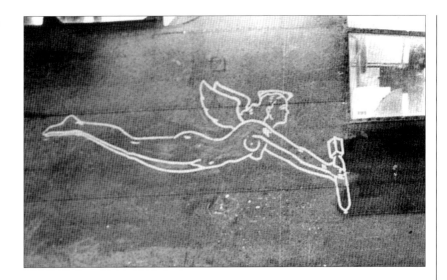

Aircraft #40-2249 was piloted by Capt Ross Greening, and would bomb Yokohama. The crew later had to bail out over China. (US Navy)

Navy deck hands ensured the B-25Bs were tied down securely to reduce any damage during the voyage. Aircraft maintenance and checks allowed crews to test their engines, as shown here. (US Navy)

dropped from the B-25s. Jurika also contributed his medal that he received from the Japanese during his assignment in the American embassy.

The task force did notice some signs of enemy activity. Radio detection efforts located a weather broadcasting ship at 44° 00' North longitude and 162° 00' East latitude. The location was about 500 miles from the Kurils, 750 miles distant from the Aleutian Islands, and 1,200 miles away from Tokyo. The ship posed no threat to TF-16, but could be a future source of concern for a raiding party taking a more northerly route.

Meanwhile, Stillwell and Chiang continued preparations for the Chinese landing sites. Arnold had started requesting specific amounts and types of petroleum products, radio equipment, and support from Stillwell from March 16. Equipment and fuel sources were scarce at best in eastern China. Weather concerns about the use of Yushan, Kian, and Lishui were raised. Unless these airfields were inspected by American

officers (Stillwell insisted that AAF officers do so), only Kweilin and Chuchow appeared able to support a "heavy bomber operation." Because of the weather conditions and several flying mishaps, some fields were not examined. Still the mission progressed; a March 30 message to Stillwell's staff specified that "[o]ne take-off and landing only by medium bombers contemplated by operation."

Stillwell sought equipment such as multi-band transmitters (333 kilocycles to 12 megacycles), long-range direction finders (200 kilocycles to 6 megacycles), and receivers (150 kilocycles to 15 megacycles) for each landing site. Gasoline and oil sources were particularly hard to find. The Russell Standard Vacuum Oil Company in Calcutta, India sold gasoline and oil to him on March 25. Stillwell was allocated 30,000 gallons of 100-octane gasoline and 500 gallons of 120-weight oil. Stillwell had to move the fuel and oil via Pan American Airways DC-3 aircraft in five-gallon tins. He also requested more information about the reasons for this, but was denied. Arnold continued to stress the importance and secrecy of fuel and equipment movements and landing sites.

Once the fuel and oil were secured, Arnold provided detailed instructions to Stillwell for support. In a March 26 cablegram, Arnold directed that Kweilin should receive 10,000 gallons of gasoline and 100 gallons of oil and the other four airfields each should receive 5,000 gallons of gasoline and 100 gallons of oil. Stillwell was authorized to use any means to deliver the fuel and supplies to the airfields. Each landing site had to have these items by midnight April 9/10. Arnold also wanted a minimum 12-member ground service team, one of whom had to speak English. Ground crews would mark each airfield with five flares on each side of the runway and five on the runway's windward end. The crews had to be ready to accomplish these actions two hours before daybreak beginning on April 10. If flares were not available, then ground crews would use lit oil tins. Chiang received notification that up to 25 B-25s would land in China only after TF-18 had left California. Arnold notified

Stillwell that on "April 20th, special project will arrive destination." Once the planes had landed, they would be refueled and directed to Chengtu and dispersed, with the crews sent to Chungking.

Stillwell had prepared all of the airfields for operations. The Japanese had attacked several of the landing sites in early April, but damage was slight. In an April 16 message to Arnold, Stillwell reported all fuel, oil, and support was ready. Stillwell also stated ground crews would transmit a signal using the figure "57" during the same two-hour period as the flares. The signal was to be transmitted on a frequency of 333 kilocycles, 900 meters. This would aid the flyers in poor weather conditions. The ground crews and landing sites appeared ready to receive Doolittle on schedule.

## "THREE CARRIERS SIGHTED"

TF-16 proceeded on course without incident. The ships' crews practiced going to general quarters at dawn and dusk, a vulnerable time for the fleet. By April 17, the American force was about 1,000 miles east of Japan. Oilers had refueled the carriers and cruisers. Weather conditions worsened with gale winds approaching 35 knots, rough seas, and visibility limited to one or two miles. At 1439 the carriers *Hornet* and *Enterprise* along with the four cruisers proceeded westward to launch the attack. The attack force sped towards its target at speeds between 20 and 25 knots. At this point, the destroyers and oilers were left behind. This allowed the carriers and cruisers to conduct high-speed movement. Additionally, leaving the destroyers behind conserved the task force's fuel. The oilers were too slow to keep up with the rest of the fleet.

The final planning seemed complete. Doolittle's crews were prepared to launch their planes on April 19 and arrive at the Chinese airfields on the morning of the 20th – except that the planners had

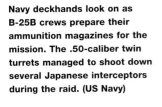

Navy deckhands look on as B-25B crews prepare their ammunition magazines for the mission. The .50-caliber twin turrets managed to shoot down several Japanese interceptors during the raid. (US Navy)

LEFT **LTC Jimmy Doolittle performed a "ceremony" on the *Hornet* to return Japanese medals "with interest." These medals were donated by US Navy veterans. (US Navy)**

BELOW **The Doolittle Raid had a great strategic impact on the Pacific Theater and World War II. Navy and Army personnel put the mission together in a mere few months. Here the crews are pictured on board the *Hornet*. (US Navy)**

failed to make time adjustments, and the dates were wrong. In the haste of completing the planning, no one had considered TF-16's crossing of the International Date Line. The mistake was discovered by TF-16 staff members, but since they were on strict radio silence nothing more could be done. If the mission proceeded as planned, Doolittle's force would arrive in China a day early. Halsey would have to radio back to Pearl Harbor once the bombers had left. Halsey never did this – but in fact it would not have helped the crews if he had.

TF-16's ships continued their vigilance against being spotted as it continued on a course of 276°. On board the *Enterprise*, a watch officer, ENS Robert Boettcher, picked up two radar contacts at 0310 on April 18. The targets were approximately 20,000 yards away at a bearing of 255°. Two minutes later, crewmen saw a light in the radar contacts' general direction. Halsey ordered all ships to general quarters. The carriers and cruisers changed course to 350° to avoid being spotted and jeopardizing the mission. By 0341 the two surface contacts drifted off the radar screen at 26,400 yards at 203°. The task force's course change succeeded in avoiding discovery and they returned to heading directly to Japan at 0415.

*Enterprise* conducted her normal aerial patrols, but with some apprehension. At 0508 combat and inner air patrols were initiated. Three Dauntless dive-bombers were launched at 0522 to search for any surface contacts. One of the planes, piloted by LT O.B. Wiseman, had seen a ship about 42 miles ahead of the task force. Wiseman believed he had been spotted and returned to the *Enterprise* and dropped a note out of his plane, to avoid radio use, to the carrier's deck indicating his finding. The task force had to change course again to 220°. However, more than a course change would be needed.

## THE NITTO MARU

At about 0744, *Hornet* lookouts spotted a Japanese picket ship 10,000 yards away bearing 221°. The ship was part of the IJN's 5th Fleet that provided an early warning system for homeland defense. The #23 *Nitto Maru* was on its normal patrol and had sighted the task force and radioed a warning at 0630 to the 5th Fleet's flagship *Kiso*. The 70-foot, 70-ton converted fishing sampan was armed with machine guns and a cannon. The IJN General Staff received notification that "[t]hree enemy carriers sighted. Position 650 nautical miles east of Inubo Saki." Doolittle was hoping to launch the attack at about 400 miles off the coast. The 5th Fleet's staff felt that an attack by an aircraft carrier would require a closer movement into Japanese waters. However, Combined Fleet headquarters transmitted quickly "[t]actical Method Number 3 against the United States Fleet" – an order to engage the enemy. Elements of the 1st and 2nd Fleets sortied out of Yokosuka and Hiroshima in search of the enemy. Vice Admiral Nagumo Chuichi's carrier force from the Indian Ocean also started towards the reported enemy carrier positions.

However, Japanese naval planners calculated that any raid would probably start early on April 19. The short range of the F4F would force the American task force to come as close as 200 miles off the coastline. Earlier Pacific Fleet carrier attacks on the Marshall and Marcus Islands

USS *Enterprise* F4F-3 Wildcats performed air cover for TF-16 throughout the mission. Here, maintenance crews test the .50-caliber machine guns. (US Navy)

A Douglas SBD Dauntless dive-bomber leads five Douglas TBD Devastator torpedo bombers off the *Enterprise.* These aircraft provided support throughout the raid. (US Navy)

had taken place from 200 miles offshore. The sighting would allow the IJN to concentrate elements of the Combined Fleet and the 5th Fleet to meet the enemy approximately 300 miles off the Japanese east coast. The IJN could surprise the attackers and deal them a death blow.

IJN operations could thus continue as normal until the next day. Yamagata, commander of the 26th Air Flotilla, had launched his normal search-aircraft patrols, twin-engine medium bombers, at 0630 from the Kisarazu Air Group. The planes, probably G4M Mitsubishi Betty aircraft, would search 700 nautical miles from the 26th's base.

In fact, the IJN was aware of a carrier force steaming in the Central Pacific, but its mission remained unknown. On April 10, Japanese Navy radio intelligence analysts had intercepted transmissions from TF-16. The naval intercepts placed the American fleet at latitude 28° 0' North and longitude 164° 0' East. The IJN staff estimated that a carrier attack on Tokyo was possible, and warned the GDC of the approach of a US Navy force. Once the *Nitto Maru*'s report had been received, the IJN reported the news to the GDC. General Prince Higashikuni's Eastern Army Command had ordered a preliminary air-raid warning to alert all air defense units. Like the IJN, the Army estimated that the carrier fleet would need to move closer and the attack would occur not earlier than the morning of April 19. The GDC could withhold the final air-raid warning until then.

Halsey ordered all ships to general quarters again after the *Nitto Maru*'s sighting. *Enterprise* Wildcats, on air combat patrols, strafed the IJN picket ship in the hope of sinking it, but failed. Dauntless dive-bombers also missed their marks. Halsey ordered the *Nashville* to attack. CAPT F.S. Craven, the *Nashville*'s commander, requested permission, by flag hoist, to open fire at 0750. Halsey approved at 0752, and a minute later the *Nashville* responded with six-inch gunfire. The *Nashville* expended an incredible 928 rounds of six-inch ammunition and took 29 minutes to sink the *Nitto Maru*. Craven put this poor performance down to gunnery-crew inexperience, heavy swells (20ft high) that complicated aiming, and initial attempts to hit the target's radio room. The ship sank at latitude 35° 50' North and longitude 153° 40' East at 0823. Crewmen saw two survivors, but they were not recovered. TF-16 was a few hundred miles short of the planned launch site and approximately eight hours early. Halsey had several choices. He could immediately retreat; push the B-25s off the deck and engage the enemy; or he could launch the attack early. Halsey made a decision to immediately launch, as planned, since TF-16 had been sighted. At 0800 the *Hornet* received orders to prepare the B-25s for take-off. Halsey's message from the *Enterprise* to Mitscher and Doolittle was "Launch Planes. To Col. Doolittle and Gallant Crew: Good Luck and God Bless You."

## "ARMY PILOTS, MAN YOUR PLANES"

The Doolittle crews prepared for their flights, after the 0800 order, earlier than expected and from a longer distance. The *Hornet* had to turn into the wind to launch the B-25s on a course of 310°. Additionally, the ordnance carried on the aircraft needed to be armed and more fuel given to the bomber crews. Navy deck crews scrambled to fill ten extra five-gallon tins (per plane) for the journey. Empty practice bombs were pressed into service as fuel containers. Navigators needed precise positions and weather conditions to plan their Japanese destinations. The bomber crews, who expected to make ready to launch their aircraft in the late afternoon, gathered to begin flight preparations. Navy deck and AAF bomber crews also had to remove the lashings that kept the aircraft from moving around the flight deck.

Conditions were not optimal for a naval aircraft launch, let alone one attempted by inexperienced land-based bomber crews. The pilots would have to contend with heavy seas, a strong northwesterly wind, and broken clouds. Waves were crashing over the decks of the cruisers and carriers.

## USS *NASHVILLE* ATTACKS JAPANESE PICKET SHIP *NITTO MARU* (pp 46–47)

Despite the extreme measures taken by Washington to ensure total secrecy about the mission, a Japanese picket ship spotted TF-16 unexpectedly early. The task force ships maintained a careful watch throughout their voyage from Alameda to Japan for any enemy naval forces or aircraft, hoping to avoid detection. Halsey's objective was to bring TF-16 as close to the Japanese home islands as possible without exposing his carriers to enemy attack. The IJN organized a flotilla of picket ships on station to provide early warning of a possible Allied raiding force. Unfortunately for Halsey and Doolittle, the *Nitto Maru* transmitted a radio message to warn Tokyo of TF-16's presence. TF-16 personnel also picked up the transmission, and Halsey launched the B-25Bs earlier than planned. The *Nitto Maru* (1), a steel sampan or fishing boat, was a converted 90-ton whaler, which had a radio, machine guns, and a small cannon. The *Nashville* (2) and aircraft from the *Enterprise* were ordered to attack the *Nitto Maru*. The attack began at 0830 on April 18, and lasted about 30 minutes. The *Nashville* used her six-inch main guns. Firing was done in salvos, three guns at a time. Douglas Dauntless SBD dive-bombers (3) and F4F Wildcats (4) from the USS *Enterprise* also bombed and strafed the sampan, but could not destroy the ship. None of the bombs dropped on the *Nitto Maru* hit the boat, and no external damage was

reported. The SBD Dauntless carried two 100-pound bombs on its wings and a single 500-pound bomb in the center fuselage. The markings (5) on the SBD in the foreground show a "B" for bomb squadron and the aircraft number identification "10". A small white identification number of the aircraft can also be seen on the cowling (6). Aircraft in the same squadrons could have different-sized roundels and markings: the US Navy issued general instructions on markings, but local variations occurred. The F4F aircraft's markings (7) "F 23" indicate "F" for fighter, and "23" for its identification number. Some aircraft from the *Enterprise* might also show a "6" in their markings, indicating they were part of the VF-6 squadron. The F4F could fire three .50-caliber machine guns per wing. The Wildcat was the US Pacific Fleet's frontline carrier fighter. Slower and less maneuverable than its nemesis, the A6M Zero, a Wildcat pilot could use the plane's rugged construction and armament to account for itself in an air-to-air encounter. On April 18, its performance against the *Nitto Maru* was less than satisfactory. The F4F would later help turn the tide of the Pacific War during the crucial Battle of Midway. The *Nitto Maru* sank rapidly after she was hit by the *Nashville*, which expended over 900 rounds in the process. The *Nashville* was also involved in another surface action, after Doolittle left the *Hornet*, to sink another picket ship. Although the *Nashville* destroyed the ship, gunnery was still poor. Halsey demanded an extensive explanation of the below average air and surface gunnery and bombing actions.

Halsey's decision to launch now had mission implications. The crews were concerned about reaching their Chinese destinations. When the bomber crews were en route to their targets coming upon the Japanese coastline, many would use Inubo Saki's lighthouse as a navigational landmark. If the distance from Inubo Saki and the carriers were 550 miles, then there would be a chance that the crews could land at all five of the prepared destinations. If the launch occurred at 650 miles, the conditions would make landing at the Yushan airfield impossible. The fleet was about 620 miles east of Inubo Saki at launch – further away than planned. According to Halsey's war diaries, he noted the crews would also be flying to Tokyo in severe weather conditions. TF-16 meteorologists clocked headwinds at speeds of 27 knots per hour, which would increase fuel consumption. The bomber crews knew that some would probably not arrive at their landing sites. In the confusion that followed, Halsey did not inform anyone about the early departure of the bombers. Also, they would attack in daylight, not in the safety of darkness.

At 0803, the *Hornet* increased speed to 22 knots to prepare for the launch. Crews heard the command: "Army pilots, man your planes." The bombers started engine warm-up procedures. Navy personnel moved the B-25s into two columns on the flight deck for take-off. Naval personnel in the *Hornet*'s control tower island provided headings and wind speeds on large signs to assist the crews and provide current information. These instructions were flashed from a gun turret. Doolittle was the first to leave the *Hornet* at 0820. TF-16's position was at latitude 35° 43' North and longitude 153° 25' East.

Launch operations proceeded with the take-off of the remaining 15 B-25s. Mitscher reported that heavy seas and wind gusts were up to 40 knots. The conditions caused the *Hornet* "to pitch violently, occasionally taking green seas over the bow and wetting the flight deck." The last flight left at 0921.

Although all planes were launched successfully, there were problems. Mitscher was very critical about the take-offs and called them "dangerous

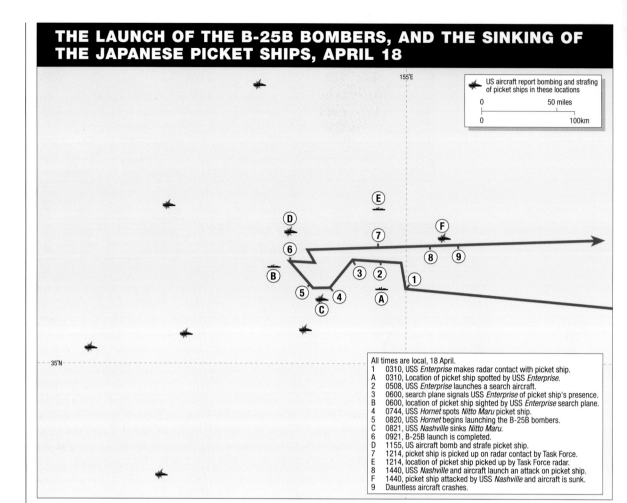

155°E

US aircraft report bombing and strafing of picket ships in these locations

0       50 miles

0       100km

35°N

All times are local, 18 April.
1   0310, USS *Enterprise* makes radar contact with picket ship.
A   0310, Location of picket ship spotted by USS *Enterprise*.
2   0508, USS *Enterprise* launches a search aircraft.
3   0600, search plane signals USS *Enterprise* of picket ship's presence.
B   0600, location of picket ship sighted by USS *Enterprise* search plane.
4   0744, USS *Hornet* spots *Nitto Maru* picket ship.
5   0820, USS *Hornet* begins launching the B-25B bombers.
C   0821, USS *Nashville* sinks *Nitto Maru*.
6   0921, B-25B launch is completed.
D   1155, US aircraft bomb and strafe picket ship.
7   1214, picket ship is picked up on radar contact by Task Force.
E   1214, location of picket ship picked up by Task Force radar.
8   1440, USS *Nashville* and aircraft launch an attack on picket ship.
F   1440, picket ship attacked by USS *Nashville* and aircraft is sunk.
9   Dauntless aircraft crashes.

and improperly executed." He witnessed aircraft with fully-back stabilizer positions during launch at the required speed. The pilot would then execute an immediate pull-up into a dangerous near stall. The B-25 crew would then struggle to gain speed; if they did not, their plane would crash. Many of the aircraft would barely keep an altitude of 100 feet. The crew's Navy instructor, LT Miller, tried to write instructions on a placard, but crews seemed to ignore the warning. Some B-25s did manage to take-off without incident by gaining speed, and "lifted gently in an easy climb and gained altitude with no trouble."

Each bomber banked right and flew over the *Hornet*, allowing each navigator to align his position. Navy navigators continued to update information to the departing B-25s. This information helped the aircraft's navigator to adjust gyroscopes and its compass. These actions were critical for calculating the flight path to the target and landing in China, especially with the additional distances and poor weather conditions.

## STRIKING THE HEART OF THE ENEMY

During the cruise towards Japan, Doolittle's crews had been given specific primary and secondary targets for the raid. The B-25s were also organized into flights of three or four aircraft, each of which would attack targets in specific geographical areas around Tokyo or further afield.

Targets were selected from AAF intelligence sources that included Tokyo, Yokohama, Kobe, Nagoya, and Osaka. In Tokyo, some of the primary targets included the Nippon Electric Company, Tokyo Gas and Electric Company, and an army arsenal. Details included a description of the target's purpose and importance to the Japanese military. For example, the Nippon Electric Company produced communications equipment, such as radios, telephones, vacuum tubes, and instruments. Intelligence officers noted that a power plant was located on the company's west side. The target was the largest communications manufacturer in Japan and employed 3,000 people. Yokohama contained several industrial targets worthy of attention such as the Ogura Oil Company, the Kawasaki Dockyard Company Aircraft Works, and the Kawasaki Aircraft Company. Nagoya was home to the Third Division Military Headquarters, a Matsushigeho Oil storage site, the Atsuta Factory that manufactured munitions, and the Mitsubishi Aircraft Works. These targets were typical of the careful selection process, which did not include civilian locations.

Doolittle organized the attack into five flights. The first flight, which included Doolittle himself, would hit northern Tokyo. The next flight was aimed at Tokyo's central sector. The third flight covered southern Tokyo. Doolittle's fourth flight was responsible for hitting southern Kanegawa, Yokohama, and the Yokosuka Navy Base. The last flight would keep its formation integrity until it was near Nagoya, before each plane flew to its final attack destinations in Nagoya, Osaka, or Kobe. Doolittle also demanded that the bombers fly in particular formations. For example, the fourth flight flew over a 50-mile front to give it maximum coverage and to deceive any Japanese observers into believing the attack was larger than its actual size. This action would also reduce the fire from

**AAF crews trained for taking off from an aircraft carrier's deck. Although the concept was proven, the densely parked aircraft represented a real problem in organizing take-offs. (US Navy)**

The *Hornet* was on her maiden voyage, and had to deliver the strike force halfway around the globe. The raid planned for only 15 aircraft to participate, but 16 took part. (US Navy)

Navy crews supported B-25B maintenance and crew training. From *Hornet*'s island on the left, instructions and signals were given to the crews during take-off. The USS *Vincennes* is in the background. (US Navy)

AAA or fighter attacks. Doolittle also thought that if the flight were spread out over a wide front, it would surprise the defenders more.

Two minutes after the launch of the Doolittle bomber force, Halsey ordered the carriers and cruisers to immediately change course to 90° and head directly east to Pearl Harbor at 25 knots. The *Enterprise* took the lead for the force. About 1107, the *Nashville* rejoined the carriers after its engagement with the *Nitto Maru*.

TF-16 did not know of enemy strength in the Tokyo area. However, the IJN's 1st Air Fleet was returning from the Indian Ocean. It included the carriers *Akagi*, *Soryu*, *Zuikaku*, *Shokaku* and *Hiryu* that was in the

Bashi Channel south of Formosa, and was steaming towards Japan. Additionally, Vice Admiral Nobutake Kondo's 2nd Fleet had returned from the Indian Ocean earlier. Its 4th and 5th Cruiser divisions were available to sortie from Yokosuka. The Combined Fleet also could rely upon five submarines from the 3rd Submarine Squadron and eight boats from the 8th Submarine Squadron. The 26th Air Flotilla and other naval units could release up to 90 Zero fighters, 80 medium bombers, 36 carrier bombers, and two flying boats. The Combined Fleet's Rear Admiral Ugaki Matome, on receipt of the *Nitto Maru*'s radio report, had ordered all available IJN ships, within a day's steaming time, to converge on the picket ship's location. Although Doolittle's planes launched earlier than expected, this was a blessing in disguise. Given the warning on April 10 and the *Nitto Maru*'s sighting, one can speculate that if TF-16's carriers and cruisers had approached closer to Japan the IJN would have been able to reach TF-16 and destroy Doolittle's bombers.

By 1030 Yamagata's patrol aircraft, which had taken off at 0630, should have reached their patrol station. No reports were received. In light of the *Nitto Maru*'s observations, Yamagata ordered another patrol of three aircraft to depart from the Misawa Air Group at 1130 to spot any enemy naval activity. Its mission was to search 700 nautical miles from Kisarazu Air Base. Still concerned, he ordered 24 Zero and 25 Kate torpedo planes to launch.

Many of Doolittle's bomber crews had earlier decorated their planes with colorful names such as "Whiskey Pete," "Whirling Dervish," "Ruptured Duck," and "Hari Kari-er." These aircraft now began their approach towards Japan. In after-action reports the crews chronicled that the waters around the Land of the Rising Sun were filled with ships of all shapes and sizes. The crews were keenly aware of the AAA and air defense interceptors facing them. Several pilots had asked Doolittle what they should do if forced to bail out over Japan. Doolittle responded he would be the last person in his plane and then fly it into the nearest target.

Doolittle's bombers flew westward toward Tokyo, taking about four hours to do so. Some planes passed ships; one was thought to be a light cruiser that was steaming east of Tokyo, and this vessel did manage to report the B-25's presence. Many patrol craft, tankers, freighters, and fishing ships were present 300 miles from the coast. There seemed to be no defensive preparations. Despite the *Nitto Maru*'s radio message, Tokyo seemed to be conducting daily business as usual.

Low clouds and rain shielded the AAF bombers until they arrived in the Tokyo area. It was clear, perfect weather for bombing. Winds and navigational errors did scatter some of the B-25s, making it difficult for the bomber crews to strike their targets. Fortunately for Doolittle's crews, the Japanese became confused, with AAF medium bombers arriving from different areas at different times, making it difficult for air defense forces to organize a counterattack. However, Japanese observation posts near Mito, about 70 miles northeast of Tokyo, reported seeing hostile bombers at 1200. Although the observation post sighting resulted in an air-raid warning message to Tokyo, the attacking B-25Bs arrived over the target city within minutes. For the next hour, Doolittle and his bomber crews would rock Tokyo and its surrounding areas.

Despite the earlier *Nitto Maru* and Mito reports, the Japanese military forces were ill-prepared to fight. Ki-27s or other aircraft could not

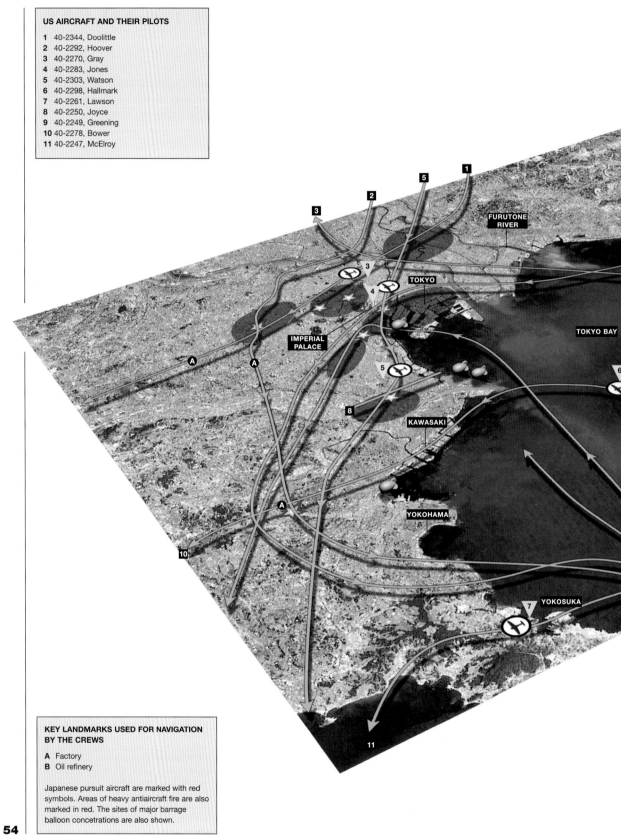

## US AIRCRAFT AND THEIR PILOTS

1 40-2344, Doolittle
2 40-2292, Hoover
3 40-2270, Gray
4 40-2283, Jones
5 40-2303, Watson
6 40-2298, Hallmark
7 40-2261, Lawson
8 40-2250, Joyce
9 40-2249, Greening
10 40-2278, Bower
11 40-2247, McElroy

## KEY LANDMARKS USED FOR NAVIGATION BY THE CREWS

A  Factory
B  Oil refinery

Japanese pursuit aircraft are marked with red symbols. Areas of heavy antiaircraft fire are also marked in red. The sites of major barrage balloon concetrations are also shown.

FURUTONE RIVER

TOKYO

TOKYO BAY

IMPERIAL PALACE

KAWASAKI

YOKOHAMA

YOKOSUKA

# THE DOOLITTLE RAID OVER TOKYO BAY

This illustration shows the paths of the planes over Tokyo Bay on April 18, 1942. The Tokyo attack was undertaken by thirteen B-25Bs. However, only the flight paths of the 11 identified aircraft over the area are shown; those of York and Holstrom are not known. There was a large concentration of shipping in Tokyo Bay at the time of the raid, including an aircraft carrier. The Doolittle planes made separate attacks at different times, but are shown here together.

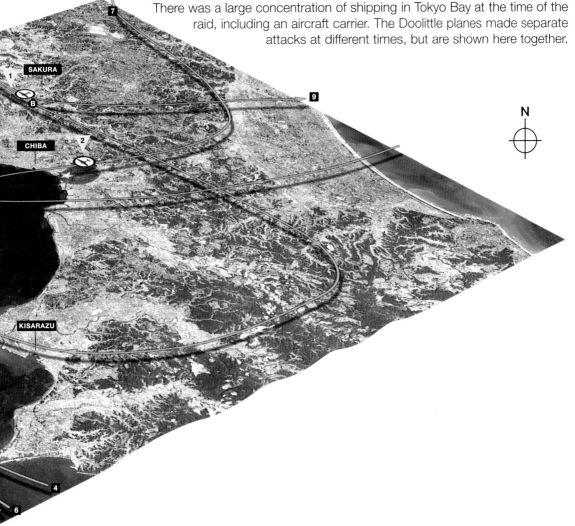

## EVENTS

1. **Four Japanese interceptor aircraft pursue 40-2249; two are shot down.**

2. **Three Japanese interceptor aircraft pursue 40-2261.**

3. **Nine Japanese interceptor aircraft pursue 40-2344 (Doolittle).**

4. **One Japanese interceptor aircraft pursues 40-2303, and is shot down.**

5. **Nine Japanese interceptor aircraft pursue 40-2303; two are shot down.**

6. **Three Japanese interceptor aircraft pursue 40-2278.**

7. **Six Japanese interceptor aircraft pursue 40-2247.**

scramble fast enough to catch the bombers. Even when they did, the
JAAF reported that the Ki-27's 7.7mm ammunition was ineffective
against the B-25; some AAF crews reported that bullets bounced off their
bomber's skin. AAA crews also complained that their fire was useless
against the low-flying attackers.

Doolittle, who was supposed to attack alone and create the incendiary
signal on Tokyo, joined the first flight of three other aircraft. They flew
on a course that would take them north of Tokyo. Doolittle's plane was
able to maintain an altitude of about 200 feet over the sea. 2Lt Richard
E. Cole, co-pilot, saw a twin-engine flying boat passing over their plane at
3,000 feet. Miraculously, the Japanese naval aircraft did not seem to
notice the B-25B, but it did report back to its headquarters about the
strange aircraft in its midst. Doolittle crossed onto Japanese territory
about 50 miles northeast of the capital and then headed southeast
towards the northeast area of Tokyo. Doolittle's crew noted many small
airfields with biplanes. These training aircraft offered little threat to the
attack force. As the plane approached to ten miles north of Tokyo, the
bomber noticed that nine pursuit planes, probably Ki-27s, were in three
formations of three aircraft apiece. Although they maneuvered for
attack, no interception was made. Doolittle guided the plane to its target
area in Toyko's east center, an armory. After the plane gained altitude to
1,200 feet, the bombardier dropped four incendiary cluster bombs at
1230. Tokyo sounded an air-raid warning after the attack. The bomb
pattern was 200 foot by 600 foot on the northeast and southwest area of
the target. AAA fire was only encountered after the plane had dropped
its ordnance. Although the AAA fire was intense, the plane escaped
destruction. The crews saw only five barrage balloons in the east central
area of Tokyo. Doolittle had achieved complete surprise. After the attack,
he headed west, and then south to the sea and on to China.

The three other aircraft in the first flight were led by 1Lt Travis
Hoover. Hoover accompanied Doolittle to Tokyo and flew to the right of
him. Like his commander, Hoover reported that his flight was not
marred by attacking pursuit planes, although he did remark that the
Japanese had a number of training planes in formation. His main target,

The B-25B had a maximum range of 2,400 miles. An earlier than expected take-off, operational issues, adverse weather conditions, and other problems forced most of the planes to ditch off the Chinese coast, or crash. (US Navy)

an Army arsenal in the center of Tokyo, was thought by Army intelligence officers to be one of Japan's largest facilities. However, they were unsure of whether it was a production plant or merely a storage base. The crew was able to locate the target between a railroad station and the Imperial Palace. Hoover's bombardier, 2Lt Richard E. Miller, started the bomb run at 900 feet since he did not have time to reach the desired 1,500-foot altitude. The crew used their three demolition weapons and one incendiary bomb against the target. Miller released the ordnance at half-second intervals, dropping them from east to west. The arsenal was struck and debris shot over the B-25. Hoover's crew did not report any AAA fire directed at his aircraft, but Hoover believed that he had seen AAA fire in the general direction where Doolittle made his run. The only possible impediment to other bombers was four to six barrage balloons south of the target at the mouth of the Tama River. The plane's escape route followed a southwesterly course through Kawasaki and Yokohama. Hoover directed the plane southeast to Tokyo Bay north of Yokosuka, then out to the open sea and on to China.

The third B-25, "Whiskey Pete," was led by 1Lt Robert M. Gray, who headed for Tokyo after leaving the carrier at 0830. His plane flew east to west, reaching firm ground due east of Yokohama. The plane then had to proceed across the Chiba peninsula and northwest across Tokyo Bay, then to Tokyo. The plane's bomb run originated slightly northwest of the Imperial Palace and proceeded at an altitude of 1,450 feet. Gray used a demolition bomb on a steel mill, but none of the crew saw the result. He then scored a direct hit on a gas company with a demolition bomb. The next target, a chemical works, also suffered a direct hit with a demolition bomb that apparently set the entire facility on fire. The last weapon dropped was an incendiary bomb that landed in a factory area.

On his route out, Gray saw three to four barrage balloons over Tokyo Harbor. The crew also used their forward nose machine gun to attack a military barracks. Again, his aircraft was not molested by pursuit planes or AAA. Gray succeeded in flying south of Tokyo Bay and on to China.

The last plane from the first flight was not as fortunate as the other three aircraft. 1Lt Everett W. Holstrom's B-25B was able to leave the *Hornet* at 0833. However, Holstrom's plane began traveling 15° off course, initially flying at an altitude of about 75 feet. The earlier flights had largely avoided the IJN and GDC defenses, but they were now alerted to the bombings. A crew member found that their left wing gas tank had sprung a leak. The deviated course compounded the problem; the plane was 80 miles from its intended landfall due to the mistake. As the plane approached near the mouth of Tokyo Bay the crew wanted to strike their primary target, but realized they would have to expend more of their dwindling fuel to do so. Holstrom's navigator, 2Lt Harry C. McCool reported in his post-attack interview that their plane was attacked by "two

## GREENING'S B-25B SHOOTS DOWN TWO KI-61 AIRCRAFT ON THE WAY TO YOKOHAMA (pp 58–59)

Captain C. Ross Greening's B-25B, nicknamed "Hari Kari-er" (1), shot down two Ki-61 Hien aircraft (2 and 3) during its bombing run, shortly after crossing Kasumigawa Lake. The B-25B crew could not positively identify the type of aircraft shot down in its initial reports, but later recognized them as Ki-61 planes after talking to intelligence officers. Aircraft 40-2249 featured distinctive nose art (4), and had fake twin .50-caliber guns in its tail (5). Four Ki-61 aircraft approached Greening's aircraft during its bombing run, two on the right and two on the left of the plane. At this time the Ki-61s were in an evaluation phase, based at Mito, and were in a natural metal finish with no markings of note save the red "meatball" roundel (6). The Ki-61 had twin 0.50-caliber machine guns in its nose and a 20mm cannon in each wing. Greening's bombing run took place shortly after noon. The B-25B used the top turret (7) to shoot down the aircraft. One Ki-61 caught fire, and went into a steep climb, while the other headed off into a dive. The crew did not see the aircraft hit the ground. Greening and his crew went on to attack an oil refinery and storage facility, despite being chased by the two remaining Ki-61s. The Ki-61 Hien resulted from Tokyo gaining access to the German Daimler-Benz 601A aircraft engine. This powerful

motor allowed the Japanese to build this new interceptor. This aircraft, compared to contemporary Japanese combat airplanes, was heavily armed; it had an armored cockpit, self-sealing fuel tanks, and achieved higher speeds than the Zero. The introduction of new aircraft would bolster the home island's air defenses. However, US AAF and Navy aircraft would not challenge Japan's air defenses until late in the war. Despite being given years to prepare for such an eventuality, the Japanese could not stop the bombing offensive, which would destroy many parts of the nation. Despite the inferior armament of the modified B-25B used by Greening's crew, his gunner managed to down two Hiens. The B-25B was able to outrun the surviving Ki-61s. The B-25B was the first B-25 version to use a power-driven gun turret. The ventral and top turrets proved difficult to use. Crews had to forgo the ventral turret due to continuing hydraulic and power problems. Mid-Continent Airlines personnel replaced the retractable ventral turret with a metal cover and used the excess space for additional fuel storage. Several Doolittle crews reported problems with rotating the turrets and having the guns jam during their mission. The "Hari Kari-er" and its crew eventually bombed a Yokohama oil refinery, dock, and industrial warehouse area. Greening survived the raid and he later served in Europe, where he became a prisoner of war of the Germans.

Japanese fighter planes. These planes resembled spitfires [sic], had elliptical wings, sharp noses, single motors." This was probably the Kawasaki Ki-61 Hien. There were twelve prototypes built by December 1941 and over 30 production aircraft flying by 1942. These aircraft may have been assigned to the numerous training fields for field evaluation and preparation for full-scale production in the coming years. The B-25 crew's problems were compounded when they discovered the top gun turret failed to operate due to an electrical system malfunction.

Holstrom's mission was endangered. His crew only had the .30-caliber nose gun and two wooden, fake machine guns placed in the rear of all the planes to create a false threat to any interceptors. The two enemy fighters were joined by two other aircraft attacking "Whiskey Pete." Almost defenseless, off course, and leaking fuel, the only sensible option was to outrun the interceptors. Holstrom decided he had to drop his three demolition bombs and one incendiary cluster to gain speed. The bombardier dropped them in Tokyo Bay and the plane flew at 270 miles per hour at full throttle. The B-25 escaped the fighters since their estimated speed was between 200 and 250 miles per hour. Two more Japanese aircraft joined the pursuit, but the B-25 continued south towards a landing in the east.

Capt David M. Jones led the second flight to the central Tokyo targets. His mission began with an 0837 take-off. The navigator, 2Lt Eugene F. McGurl, charted an east–west course in which the plane arrived northeast of Tokyo. The crew had a difficult time finding landmarks to chart the course. AAA fire also caused more confusion. The plane then headed parallel to Yokosuka by turning south and then west to the opening of Tokyo Bay. The bomb run would have to come up Tokyo Bay into an area near the Imperial Palace. Navy aircraft handlers had fueled all B-25s before take-off, but leakage and evaporation took its toll. Jones now suffered from the extended range, confusion about landmarks, and his less than full fuel tanks. He believed he could not risk flying around Tokyo to attack any of his assigned targets, an armory one mile north of the Imperial Palace and another in a densely populated area.

Jones had to make attacks against targets of opportunity. The plane was southeast of the Imperial Palace. He ordered the bombardier, 2Lt Denver V. Truelove, to "cabbage" a demolition bomb from 1,200 feet on a large oil tank south of the Imperial Palace about two city blocks from the waterfront. The crew reported that the bomb made a direct hit. The next available target appeared to be a brick power plant or foundry that had many chimneys. A demolition bomb destroyed the entire building. Jones then banked the aircraft to a westerly course and the crew selected a large building that looked like a manufacturing plant. The building encompassed two city blocks by one city block. Crew members remembered that the target had a saw-toothed roofed building with new wings. In their after-action mission report, Jones' crew remarked that the building reminded them of the North American aircraft plant, the makers of the B-25. The incendiary bomb used in the attack covered the building's roof and a few of the four-pound cluster bombs bounced off the roof onto paved areas alongside the building. Jones selected the last demolition bomb for a two-story building. Unfortunately, the B-25 was traveling at 260 to 270 miles per hour and Truelove, in charge of the plane during a bomb run, overshot the target. Instead, another target was found. It was a "fairly new rectangular building with windows and ventilators on the roof" that had a canal to its west and encompassed half a city block. All of the targets were within a mile of each other. Fortunately for Jones' crew, the intense AAA fire did not hit their plane. All of the enemy fire was behind or to the sides of the B-25. Jones avoided some barrage balloons and the AAA fire, and headed southwest out of the area.

Following Jones' flight off the carrier was 1Lt Dean Hallmark, whose plane, dubbed the "Green Hornet," left for Tokyo at 0837. Hallmark's plane was destined to attack the Central Tokyo Steel Mill. According to Hallmark's navigator, Chase J. Nielsen, the first attack against the target did not entirely destroy it. Hallmark decided to circle the target again and bomb it a second time. It destroyed the steel mill.

The last plane from the second flight was 1Lt Ted W. Lawson's "Ruptured Duck." Lawson's exploits began with a launch from the

Navy aircraft handlers repositioned the B-25Bs to free deck space for take-off. This image shows the third or fourth aircraft to leave the *Hornet*. (US Navy)

*Hornet* at 0843. Lawson took the "Ruptured Duck" on an east to west course, heading northeast of Tokyo near Kasumigawa Lake. Like earlier flights, the plane saw many small vessels and ships within 400 miles of the coast. Lawson's aircraft carried the demolition bomb that contained the returned IJN medals. One crew member inscribed the bomb with the statement "I don't want to set the world on fire – just Tokyo!" The B-25, upon landfall, turned southwest to an approach on the east side of Tokyo Bay. The course appeared to be the same as Jones's plane. Lawson's crew did see six pursuit aircraft in formation overhead at 11,000 to 12,000 feet, but they did not break formation to attack the plane. The crew also saw an aircraft carrier at anchor in the bay.

Lawson's course took him south of Tokyo near the waterfront. His bombing approach came from east to west. Co-pilot 2Lt Dean Davenport reported that he could see "very large" Tokyo fires in the direction of where Doolittle had attacked. The Tokyo area was becoming covered in a smoky haze, but the area south of the city still had relatively good visibility. The original target was the Nippon Machine Works. AAA fire, top gun turret problems, and the presence of pursuit fighters prompted Lawson to lower his altitude. His crew could not find their primary target, and instead bombed several factories near the waterfront.

Flying at 1,400 feet, Davenport believed that the plane dropped its first demolition bomb, a direct hit, on a railroad and locomotive factory. However, after-action reports on Lawson's flight indicated that it was actually a large steam plant or powerhouse that was about one-half to a single city block in size. The target had four chimneys about 100 feet high on its flat roof. The building was made of cement and wood, indicating it was an industrial target. The navigator, 2Lt Robert S. Clever, identified this target in prewar photographs in intelligence files as a large steam-power plant. Another crew member did not recall any railroad tracks leading up to the target. The next target was a factory that was described

Doolittle Raiders started their take-offs from the *Hornet* at 0820 on April 18. Flying off a rolling carrier deck was a new experience for the crews. (US Navy)

This photograph shows the rough sea conditions and overcast weather at the time of take-off. The tail guns were wooden dummies, intended to frighten any Japanese fighters. (US Navy)

as "long and low" with a few small chimneys sticking out of a peaked roof. The third target was also a suspected factory, but larger than the second target. Lawson dropped the single incendiary bomb in an area southeast of the Imperial Palace. The crew could not identify a particular structure. They reported that the target was in a heavily populated area. The plane escaped unscathed after the attack.

The last flight of bombers assigned to strike Tokyo was led by Capt Edward J. "Ski" York. York's plane left the *Hornet* at 0846. He had served as Doolittle's operations officer during the training at Eglin. The compressed training schedule, secrecy, and complex training had forced York to miss much of the training himself. Unbeknownst to York, the unauthorized adjustments to carburetors made by the Sacramento Air Depot would affect his aircraft. Sacramento maintenance crews had replaced two carburetors in York's B-25 and this problem was not discovered until an investigation after the raid.

York and his crew reached the Japanese coastline, but had difficulty locating Tokyo. They were also running short of fuel. York thus decided to attack targets of opportunity. He found a factory with several railroad tracks leading from it. The building appeared to be a manufacturing site since it had four chimney stacks and appeared to be a three-story facility. York reached a 1,500-foot altitude and released the three demolition weapons and one incendiary bomb on the single target.

The crew's only concern was the high rate of gasoline consumption. York estimated that they did not have sufficient fuel to reach the Chinese coast. They would be short by 300 miles. York's options were to reach Korea, which was held by the Japanese, or disregard Doolittle's direct order not to land in the Soviet Union. Landing in Korea would mean capture or an arduous journey through enemy territory. Instead, York decided to head north to the Soviet Union.

Following York's aircraft off the *Hornet* was 1Lt Harold F. Watson's "Whirling Dervish," also destined for the Tokyo area. At 0850, Watson began his long journey west. The flight to Japan was uneventful, and the plane maintained a 500-foot altitude until it reached the coastline. York then pulled the plane up to 4,500 feet. By the time "Whirling Dervish" reached Tokyo from the northeast, the Japanese defenders were ready to hurl AAA at any B-25; intense fire was received. The crews also saw several airfields. On one airfield, Watson's co-pilot 2Lt James Parker, Jr. noted: "twenty 2-engine bombers were dispersed and fifteen or twenty pursuits warming up on a ramp."

The main target selected was the Tokyo Gas and Electric Engineering Company. The target was located on a sand spit that appeared to have several building complexes. These buildings ran north to south and had at least two saw-tooth patterned roofs. Watson positioned his plane to attack from the northeast. He had used the Imperial Palace, waterways, bridges, and railway lines to approach the target. Watson's crew then used reference points such as six parallel rail lines, the Shiagawa rail yard, the approximate location of the waterfront to the target, the Japan Special Steel Company (located on an island), a large gas tank, and Haneda airport. The identification of these reference points and the target was made while at an altitude of 2,500 feet and traveling at speeds from 220 to 230 miles per hour. Like previous crews, they also saw numerous fires throughout Tokyo and intense AAA fire as they began their bomb run. AAA sites were sighted north of the Imperial Palace and the ground fire increased as the plane traveled towards Tokyo Bay.

"Whirling Dervish" released all of its demolition bombs and incendiary cluster munitions against this single target. An observer aboard the "Whirling Dervish" saw only one demolition bomb strike the northernmost building in the group. While the crew bombed, a Japanese pursuit plane attacked the B-25 from the rear. T/Sgt Eldred V. Scott, acting as engineer-gunner, reported a radial motor, unpainted, all-metal aircraft had approached from underneath the aircraft to about 100 yards to the rear of the B-25. The plane also had a retractable

## MCELROY BOMBS THE AIRCRAFT CARRIER *RYUHO* AT YOKOSUKA NAVAL BASE (pp 66–67)

The greater Tokyo area contained many political, economic, and military targets for the AAF to select, one of which was Yokosuka. The IJN used Yokosuka as a major naval facility for ship repair and other fleet activities. A single B-25B, number 40-2247 (1), piloted by 1Lt Edgar E. McElroy struck the naval base, which was located on the western side of Tokyo Bay, south of Tokyo city. The attack achieved excellent results, particularly in damaging the aircraft carrier *Ryuho* (2), a submarine tender being converted into a carrier. One bomb hit the side of the ship, and it burst into flames. The ship was in a floating dry dock at the time, and listed to one side after the explosion. A loading crane (3) was also destroyed in the attack, breaking into a "thousand pieces" in the sky. In addition, workshops and buildings in the vicinity were hit using an incendiary device that showered down some 125 four-pound bombs. This started multiple fires in the wooden workshop and on the warehouse roofs. The pilot noted there was a lot of smoke and fire after the

attack. McElroy also recalled that he had to duck behind a hill to avoid heavy anti-aircraft fire in the vicinity of Yokosuka. AAF and Navy maintenance crews loaded the B-25B bombers with a combination of 500-pound demolition bombs and cluster bombs containing incendiary munitions. Despite their relatively small payloads, most of the Doolittle bombers, including McElroy's, achieved impressive results. Japanese building materials contributed to bomb damage, being mostly wood, not masonry. Demolition and incendiary devices proved deadly against the structures. The Yokosuka Kaigin Kosho shipbuilder operated the navy base's dry-dock that contained the *Ryuho*. The carrier would be completed in November 1942, and would carry up to 31 aircraft, with a displacement of 13,360 tons. The hurried repairs and construction required workers to use electrical welding, which would weaken its structural integrity. IJN personnel surrounded the *Ryuho* at Kure when the nation surrendered in 1945. The attack on the *Ryuho* provided a visible reminder to the IJN and the Japanese nation that they were at risk from a strike despite the apparent weakness of American and Allied military forces in 1942.

landing gear and fired tracer rounds from what appeared to be four machine guns in the wings. As the aircraft gained 500 feet in altitude and positioned itself another 300 feet back, Scott opened fire with the rear turret's twin machine guns. Scott hit the enemy aircraft, probably a Zero or Hien, and its wing fell off. The attacker was not seen again nor did it manage to hit Watson's craft.

Watson crossed into Tokyo Bay and escaped. The crew also saw few ships, but did observe a battleship and two cruisers east of Kyushu Island. Scott noted that the battleship opened fire with not only AAA fire, but with her "heavy guns." The crew saw three or four white puffs from the AAA and saw gushing columns of water where the heavy-caliber shells fell back into the bay. Curiously, the cruisers did not add to the AAA fire. Another of Doolittle's bombers had once again successfully defied Japanese defenses. "Whirling Dervish" headed south, then east towards the Chinese coast.

The last B-25 mission scheduled for Tokyo was led by 1Lt Richard O. Joyce. Joyce and crew departed *Hornet* at 0853 and flew at 500 feet towards the coast. The aircraft then ascended to an altitude of 3,000 feet. His primary target was the Japan Special Steel Company plants and warehouses located in southern Tokyo. The target was located a mile and a half north of the Tana River. If the plane could not strike the primary target, its secondary mission was to level any industrial targets within reach. One factory that the crew sought was a factory that made precision instruments.

Coincidently, Joyce's crew was not supposed to take part in the raid. His aircraft and crew were supposed to return to Alameda after the *Hornet* had left San Francisco and out of observable sight, following the demonstration flight from the carrier deck. Instead, it became part of the raid.

Succeeding AAF aircraft faced an onslaught of heavier AAA fire and aroused fighter interceptors. Joyce's aircraft was no exception. The AAF bomber struck the target at 2,500 feet. Fortunately, the AAA fire missed

his plane and he delivered at least two demolition bombs on the steel manufacturer, causing heavy damage. The other demolition and incendiary bomb fell in the industrial area of Shiba. These last two munitions exploded in a densely populated area.

Although Joyce had bombed the target and escaped AAA hits, he did not entirely avoid enemy fighters. Some of Joyce's crew reported that up to nine Zero fighters harassed the B-25 from below, to the rear, in front, and above the struggling bomber while the bomb run was taking place. The bomber received hits in the fuselage and the tail area, causing an eight-inch gash forward of the horizontal stabilizer. However, the plane was not defenseless and the rear turret gunner S/Sgt Edwin W. Horton, Jr. reported that he shot down one Japanese pursuit plane. Later, Horton claimed another Japanese interceptor to his guns; tracer rounds hit their mark and the aircraft's wing.

Joyce tried to use the B-25's speed to out-race the pursuit aircraft. He put the craft into a dive and started to reach a speed of 337 miles per hour and left the pursuit planes trailing well behind. The combination of speed and the fake rear guns may have helped scare off the aircraft for a while – except for one last attack. During Joyce's flight out of Tokyo, a last interceptor tried to shoot down the B-25. The damaged bomber's engines powered the craft into a climb that the pursuing aircraft could not match. A carrier in Tokyo Bay also fired its AAA at the fleeing plane, but without success. Joyce and crew settled back into their trip to China.

By 1245, the remaining aircraft from the IJN's 26th Air Flotilla were ordered airborne to search for the American carriers and intercept any attacking bombers flying to Tokyo. Kisarazu and Tateyama naval air fields were abuzz with Mitsubishi Betty bombers and Zero fighters. The IJN ground crews armed the Betty bombers with torpedoes. The Kisarazu Air Group launched 16 Betty bombers, while the Misawa Air Group got eight into the air and the 4th Air Group managed to send only five planes. The 6th Air Group and the ground detachment from the *Kaga* contributed 12 Zero fighters, equipped with extra fuel tanks.

The fourth Doolittle flight was primed to attack targets around Tokyo Bay, but not the capital city. In 1942, there were several lucrative

Each B-25B would take-off, then circle to the right over the aircraft carrier to receive last-minute navigational information. (US Navy)

The entire launch sequence took about an hour. The last B-25B left at 0921. (US Navy)

military and industrial targets located near the bay. Capt C. Ross Greening was assigned to lead his crew out towards Yokohama, the industrial center of Japan, at 0856. Greening's journey to Japan was uneventful, but a 25-knot headwind was forcing him to use more fuel than expected. Slight navigation errors caused his plane "Hari Kari-er" to approach landfall north of his original course, northeast of Tokyo, and proceed past Kasumigawa Lake. He stayed on the eastern side of the greater Tokyo area.

After crossing the lake, "Hari Kari-er" passed an active JAAF airfield on its southerly flight to Yokohama. Ten minutes later, four interceptors attacked Greening's plane. He described the planes as "new model fighters closely resembling Zeros except [with] inline engines." Greening estimated that the four planes had a top speed of 260 miles per hour with

six wing-mounted machine guns. In his 1948 Armed Forces Staff College monograph on the raid, Greening claimed the planes were proven to be Ki-61 Hien aircraft. They were attacked, but the first pursuit aircraft was hit by the turret gunner, Sgt Melvin J. Gardner; he reported the attacker "wobbled off" and later crashed. The second Japanese plane was hit by Gardner and was seen in flames. Neither plane was seen hitting the ground. Gardner ran out of ammunition, and the two remaining Japanese aircraft caused light damage to the B-25.

Greening's primary target was an oil refinery and storage area that was camouflaged, but his crew easily spotted it, even at low altitude. The Japanese oil refinery workers had tried to put a thatched roof on the tanks and other buildings to deceive any air threat, but Greening was not fooled. The two remaining fighters had stayed with "Hari Kari-er" and forced Greening to lower his altitude to 600 feet; he outran them after the attack. The bombardier S/Sgt William L. Birch dropped four incendiary bombs on the target. Immediately after dropping the bombs, the B-25 crew felt the explosion's shock waves. As Greening brought "Hari Kari-er" to a southeasterly course, crew members remarked that they saw a large column of smoke from the target, visible for up to 50 miles. During his retreat from the area, Greening tried to sink three small boats, each about 50 to 60 feet in length, near the eastern mouth of Tokyo Bay. The .30-caliber machine-gun fire was effective. One ship was seen burning.

The twelfth plane in the attack, "Fickle Finger," was piloted by 1Lt William M. Bower. Bower left the *Hornet* at 0859, and stayed in formation with Greening, since both were assigned to attack Yokohama. However, once they reached the Japanese coastline, they separated and headed for their targets. Bower reached Chosi, a city east of Tokyo, and then flew in a southerly direction following the east coastline. Bower noted a JAAF airfield across Tokyo Bay from Yokohama some 20 miles inland. He believed he saw 20–50 aircraft, but they never took to the air; they were probably training aircraft. The crew then found themselves east of Yokohama and could see a large fire in the direction of the tank farm attacked by Greening.

On the approach to Yokohama, three Japanese pursuit aircraft followed Bower for several miles. The interceptors never approached closer than 1,000 yards, and did not attack "Fickle Finger." The B-25 passed south of the IJN's Kisarazu Naval Air Station in order to approach Yokohama from the northeast. Kisarazu appeared deserted, since the IJN had earlier sent its aircraft east in search of TF-16 and the AAF bombers.

Bower's navigator, 2Lt William Pound, had no difficulty identifying key landmarks like the naval air station or Kawasaki waterfront. Bower's original target was the Yokohama dockyards. The Japanese had also realized the importance of this key industrial site that supported the IJN and commercial shipping. They had placed five barrage balloons around it. Three balloons were at 1,500 feet and the other two at 2,500 to 3,000 feet. AAA fire, from hills west of the target, shot down some of the balloons. Bower decided to attack his secondary target, the Ogura Refinery. "Fickle Finger" was flying at about 1,100 feet with an air speed of about 200 miles per hour, preparing to drop one demolition bomb on the oil refinery. Within a range of half a mile, the bomber crew released the rest of their ordnance. Two demolition bombs struck factories and warehouses west of the Ogura Refinery. Bower and Pound saw the second and third bombs hit one corner of a building and a railroad siding between two other buildings. The last weapon, an incendiary bomb, was aimed at a warehouse west of the second and third targets. After dropping their bombs, the crew noticed a power station southwest of their attack. Bower's crew decided to machine gun the building. The .30-caliber nose gun hit the building and transformers, making sparks fly. About 100 miles east of the coastline, the crew again used its nose gun to sink a weather ship.

The last plane in the fourth flight was 1Lt Edgar E. McElroy's B-25, which was tasked with making an attack on the Yokosuka Naval Base located on the eastern half of Tokyo Bay. The mission began with an 0901 take-off, and like Bower's flight McElroy flew in formation with

# THE ATTACK ON NAGOYA BY 40-2297

The Doolittle Raid did not only strike targets in the immediate vicinity of Tokyo; other bombing attacks occurred around Japan. Three United States Army Air Forces B-25Bs were assigned targets in Osaka, Kobe, and Nagoya. The expansion of the target set allowed the raid to spread the initial shock even wider. This illustration shows the attack on Nagoya. Unlike the Tokyo raid, only two US B-25B aircraft attacked Nagoya, one of which was meant to attack the prime target of Osaka but lost its bearings. Unfortunately, the track of the latter's flight path was lost forever when the logbook was destroyed after the Japanese captured the crew, and so only one flight path, that of Hilger's plane, is shown here.

US AIRCRAFT

1   40-2297, Hilger

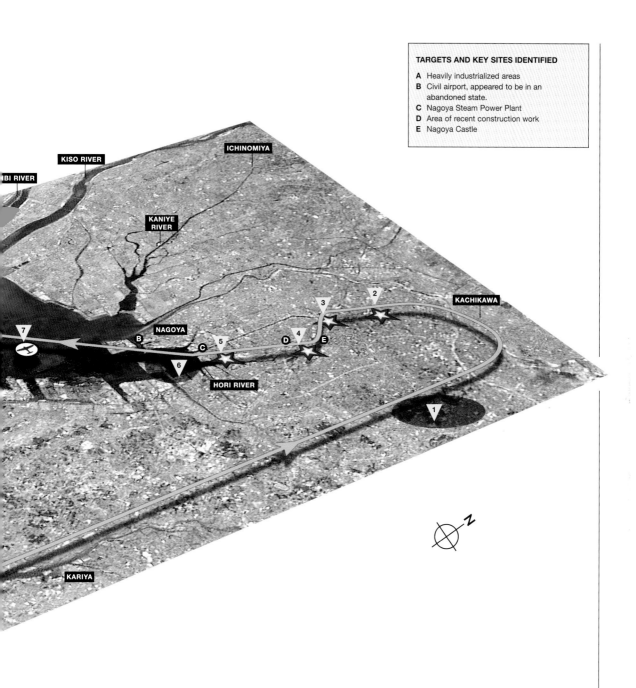

IBI RIVER

KISO RIVER

ICHINOMIYA

KANIYE RIVER

KACHIKAWA

NAGOYA

HORI RIVER

KARIYA

▼ EVENTS

1. **Heavy antiaircraft fire encountered in this area.**

2. **Military barracks building bombed.**

3. **Oil storage facilities hit.**

4. **Atsuta Aircraft Factory bombed.**

5. **Mitsubishi Aircraft Works bombed.**

6. **Heavy antiaircraft fire encountered in this area.**

7. **Japanese Ki-26 interceptor aircraft sighted in pursuit of 40-2297, but does not attack.**

McElroy's B-25B damaged a Japanese aircraft carrier in dry dock and destroyed some of the Yokosuka shipyard. (Air Force Historical Research Agency)

flight leader Capt Greening. When Greening and Bower separated to their assigned courses toward Yokohama, McElroy had to find his own way to the navy base. Yokosuka was homeport for several IJN ships and contained repair docks for the fleet. The Japanese air defenses were delivering concentrated and heavy AAA fire and they zeroed in on McElroy as he passed the Tokyo area. Fortunately, his aircraft was not spotted by any pursuit aircraft.

McElroy decided to quickly strike Yokosuka's dock area. Several ships in repair occupied the dockyard. Flying at an altitude of 1,500 feet, the B-25 prepared to unleash its bomb load on the docks and support facilities. One bomb struck a large ship-loading crane, which collapsed and the crew considered it destroyed. The other munitions hit a ship that appeared to be an aircraft carrier. Yokosuka dock workers had taken a submarine tender, *Taigei*, into the facility on December 18, 1941, and IJN headquarters authorized the conversion of it into the aircraft carrier *Ryuho*. The B-25's crew members recalled seeing the *Ryuho* falling to its side after the attack; a demolition bomb had hit the ship. Ironically, *Ryuho* was eventually completed, but only took part in one major operation, the Marianas, and was scrapped in 1946. Another ship was seen burning while it was refueling. Support facilities were set alight after McElroy hit them with an incendiary bomb.

The only surviving photographs from the raid came from co-pilot 2Lt Richard A. Knobloch. Some aircraft, notably flight leader planes, had cameras installed to record the impact of the bombing raids. Unfortunately, none of the film survived except from Knobloch's efforts. Knobloch had purchased a camera at the Sacramento Air Depot to take his own photographs and these were the only combat shots that reached home. He even took a picture of a ship 200 miles off the Japanese coast.

The last flight from the *Hornet* was dedicated to areas other than Tokyo Bay. Maj John A. Hilger was set to hit Nagoya, about 20 miles southeast of

Tokyo. Hilger's plane had no difficulty leaving the *Hornet* at 0907. The crew did spot a patrol plane, perhaps a flying boat, about 600 miles east of Tokyo, that was cruising east at 2,000 to 3,000 feet. The B-25 flew east of Yokosuka on the coast and followed it around Tokyo Bay. The flight to Nagoya then passed Oshima Island, south of Tokyo Bay's mouth, and reached a position where Hilger could make his southern attack run. The plane had dropped in altitude to around "15 to 20 feet" according to the co-pilot, 2Lt Jack A. Sims. Sims remembered that the plane maintained that altitude from the time their plane reached landfall near Nagoya, until it reached a series of hills south of the city. He set a course where he would fly up an inlet east of Nagoya, bypass it and then turn around and start the bomb run heading north to south. The crew encountered some AAA fire as it prepared to turn and attack Nagoya.

The aircraft had four incendiary bombs. Hilger hoped to drop a bomb each on the Third Military Division Headquarters (next to Nagoya Castle); the Atsuta Factory in the Nagoya Arsenal in the center of the city; the Matsushigeho Oil storage northwest of the business district; and the Mitsubishi Aircraft Works on the waterfront. For the strike, Hilger's crew set altitude at 1,500 feet and maintained airspeed at 205 miles per hour. The navigator, 2Lt James H. Macia, Jr. recalled that Nagoya's landmarks were less conspicuous than expected. Macia had difficulties identifying some of them, especially canals and waterways, from the charts. He did manage to locate some other landmarks, such as a graveyard, radio towers, the Nagoya Steam Power Plant, and others. The B-25 flew over an airport and the only planes on the field were two obsolete bombers. The airfield that Hilger's crew did spot seemed to be in a state of disrepair. It was narrow and short, and incapable of generating many sorties.

The first target, the military headquarters, was struck across a set of main barracks with the first bomb. The crew had problems locating Nagoya Castle since it did not stand out – nor did another landmark, a river that was north of the castle, which had dried up. Crew members identified the other three targets without much trouble. Next on the target list was the Matsushigeho Oil storage. Although Hilger never saw any oil storage tanks, he dropped an incendiary bomb on a large set of buildings. Macia had known that this target consisted of a set of warehouses, so it was not unusual to see many buildings other than oil tank storage. Hilger picked the largest building in the group; it resembled a college gymnasium with a curved roof. The B-25 crew struck the largest building at the Atsuta Factory. This target, according to Macia, had expanded with additional facilities compared to the pre-flight intelligence reports. The last target was the Mitsubishi Aircraft Works. The Japanese had built the plant with concrete and steel construction or masonry that did not appear vulnerable to an incendiary device. However, the surrounding residential area was composed of homes built of light wood. Intelligence officers noted this report in the after-action interviews perhaps for future reference in attacks that would consume Japan.

After bomb release, Hilger's crew suffered a heavy AAA attack at the plane's rear, but was not damaged. The plane dropped to an altitude of 200 to 300 feet to reduce its vulnerability to AAA. The attack occurred about three or four miles south of Nagoya. Hilger also managed to use his plane's nose gun to strafe an oil tank farm. An enemy interceptor appeared through the AAA smoke burst, but it did not attack since the

B-25 outran its pursuit and flew its escape route. As the crew left, they could see fires raging from the targets that they had just hit. A column of smoke, in the shape of a mushroom cloud, arose to 5–6,000 feet, marking a successful raid. Reports from Chinese radio sources after the attack claimed that the Nagoya fires burned for 48 hours after Hilger's bomb run. On the way out, Hilger and crew spotted some IJN ships, three cruisers and two destroyers off the coast of Kyushu. The ships did not fire upon the B-25. Hilger followed a southwesterly course, but attempted to lead any Japanese observers to believe they were headed out to sea, possibly to land on a carrier. After 20 minutes on the course, the plane changed direction to follow the coast and make for China.

1Lt Donald Smith's aircraft also headed for Nagoya with Hilger. The fifteenth aircraft to leave the *Hornet* (at 0915) would follow Hilger, but would separate and head west towards the port city of Kobe. It had a special crew member, the medical officer Lt White, in case anyone needed help after landing. His fellow crew would need his invaluable services after the attack.

Smith followed Hilger until he continued past Nagoya Bay and west towards Osaka. The crew was surprised when a 2,500-foot mountain, four miles northeast of Osaka, was observed that was not identified in any of the aerial charts. The crew had to take evasive actions to miss the mountain and they became concerned that they were off course. Once the crew headed west, they identified Osaka to the southwest and continued to Kobe. This event was not unusual among aircrews; the aerial charts given to Doolittle's command had numerous errors or omissions that put doubt in the crews' minds and may have led to false target identification or navigational errors.

Smith's aircraft was armed with four incendiary bombs. The approach onto Kobe would follow the coastline to the city's eastern edge and then hit targets near the waterfront. They would then head in a southwesterly route to the open sea. Smith's crew saw many small fishing ships, freighters, and other vessels in Nagoya Bay. No enemy interceptors were observed. The only aviation activity was from a DC-3-type commercial aircraft flying east of Osaka. The densely populated area between Osaka and Kobe was obscured by a smoky haze from the area's heavy industrial activity. However, as the aircraft flew east, visibility around Kobe improved and crew members clearly identified many of the appropriate landmarks that led them to the targets.

Smith was able to attack four primary targets. The crew witnessed a large aircraft carrier under construction in Osaka, but passed it by to concentrate on their primary targets. The first target was the Uyenoshita Steelworks, near a series of piers on the waterfront. The crew then turned its attention to the Kawasaki Dockyard at Point Kawa where another large aircraft carrier was well under construction. Continuing on its southwesterly trajectory, the bomber struck the Electric Machinery Works. The surrounding area near the target had numerous machine shops, small industrial factories, and residential sites. Smith spent the last bomb on the Kawasaki Aircraft Factory and Kawasaki Dockyard Company Aircraft Works #10 and #11. Smith's after-action report noted numerous factories and possible targets for future bombing raids in the area. One target in particular was a new aircraft factory east of Kobe.

Surprisingly, Smith's crew faced little opposition from the Japanese. The sudden bombing raid caught the city's defense by surprise. The B-25 was attacked, only after it had dropped its bombs, by two AAA guns as it headed out to Nagoya Bay. The two AAA guns had enough time to fire only two to three rounds, and Smith's plane was not hit. The plane headed due south out of Kobe and intersected the southern tip of Kyushu Island. There were some signs of enemy activity in the vicinity. Smith's crew reported seeing three enemy cruisers steaming on a northeast course. These ships were probably the same vessels that Watson, in "Whirling Dervish," had observed earlier. In this case, Smith did not report any hostile fire or action. However, the escaping B-25 was seen by three pursuit aircraft. Approximately 15 minutes after Smith sighted the IJN force, he noticed two pursuit aircraft performing target practice over the water. These planes tried to intercept the bomber, but their slow speed allowed Smith to outdistance them without any trouble. Sgt Edward J. Saylor, the flight engineer, identified the pursuit aircraft as Ki-27s by their fixed landing gear.

The crew advised AAF intelligence officers, in interviews after the raid, that Kobe seemed ripe for attack. These reports suggested that the city's lack of defenses and many targets made it susceptible to a dive-bombing attack that could devastate the area. Although future bombing raids on Japan proper would occur later, intelligence teams began the collection of information on potential targets. Information about AAA locations, barrage balloons, map references, and suitable targets gave planners valuable source material. Statements such as "the waterfront seemed to be packed with factories" and bombs dropped "at random could not miss" did not escape notice. The next time the Japanese GDC or IJN forces would face American bombers in Tokyo would occur on November 24, 1944 when 111 B-29s hit the Musahino aircraft plant.

The last plane off the *Hornet* was 1Lt William Farrow's "Bat out of Hell." Farrow's mission began with departure from the carrier at 0921. The heavy seas and winds that plagued carrier operations hit with a vengeance when Farrow's plane slid backwards as it prepared for take-off and the *Hornet*'s deck rolled. Unfortunately, one of the B-25's spinning propellers struck a sailor's arm, which he lost. This unfortunate accident was a sign of events to follow. Farrow's primary targets were in the Osaka area. The plane's course was relatively uneventful until it

Doolittle Raiders and TF-16 vessels sighted and attacked a number of Japanese ships like this one. Some commercial fishing ships were pressed into service by the IJN, and were armed with small-caliber cannon and machine guns. The *Nashville* and carrier aircraft had great difficulty in destroying these ships, though. (US Air Force)

reached its designated target. Heavy AAA fire around Osaka forced Farrow to change his route; instead of hitting his primary targets, he was forced to turn back on Nagoya.

AAA fire in Nagoya was concentrated and Farrow was forced to search for targets of opportunity. "Bat out of Hell" made attacks on an oil tank and an aircraft factory. Crew members witnessed a fire in the oil tank area. As the plane continued south, Cpl Jacob D. DeShazer, the bombardier, noticed several Japanese pursuit aircraft attempting to shoot down his plane. DeShazer, now that he had dropped the incendiary weapons, was free to operate the top turret. He did not fire since the B-25 was flying too fast for the Japanese pilots.

Miraculously, all 16 Doolittle bombers had escaped unscathed from the most heavily defended air space in the Japanese Empire. The only objective remaining for the crews was to try to reach the Chinese landing sites.

# TF-16'S VOYAGE HOME

Halsey's return to Pearl Harbor was not without incident. The IJN was actively pursuing the carriers, and Nimitz's worst fears of losing two carriers could still materialize. The benefit of Halsey's decision to launch Doolittle's raid earlier than expected was a head start on leaving hostile waters. TF-16 would have to elude 5th Fleet picket ships to escape detection and eventual attack by any long-range, land-based IJN aviation assets. Similarly, Halsey could not be certain that the Japanese home waters hosted carriers, submarines, or surface ships returning from Indian Ocean operations.

The IJN command was very active. The search for the American naval strike would continue until April 24. Yamagata ordered Kisarazu Air Group and Marcus Island-based aircraft to search up to 700 nautical miles for the American fleet. He also placed all aircraft at Kisarazu and Tateyama on a 15-minute alert in case his reconnaissance flights dicovered the location of the enemy or in case additional raids were forthcoming.

The *Enterprise* and *Hornet* were ready for action. All ships remained at
general quarters throughout the day. Both carriers shared duties of

launching Wildcat fighters to maintain combat air patrols. By 1115, the *Hornet* had launched eight Wildcats. Additionally, the *Enterprise* had already sent the carrier's scouting squadron Dauntless dive-bombers in 200-mile patterns to find any IJN ships that might prove hostile or could report the task force's whereabouts. *Enterprise* radar operators did detect one of Yamagata's long-range patrol planes at 1214. However, the closest the plane came to the carrier was 64,000 yards.

Fleeing east, the task force again spotted enemy forces. At approximately 1400, *Enterprise* search aircraft returning home sighted two enemy patrol craft. These picket ships were probably the same craft that radar had detected at 0310. The Dauntless bombers did manage eventually to sink one of the ships, but machine-gun fire from the patrol ships damaged a plane in its engine. That aircraft crashed off the *Nashville*, but the crew was recovered safely. The *Nashville* now concentrated on sinking the other patrol ship.

The *Nashville* had broken contact with the other task force ships at 1409 to sink both ships. Once the Dauntless dive-bombers had sunk one of the patrol craft, the *Nashville* began to close on the other target that was north of her and about 9,000 yards away. Other aircraft from the *Hornet* also strafed and bombed the remaining ship. Dive-bombers unleashed their ordnance at altitudes of 100 feet from the water. *Nashville* proceeded and approached the wooden, 90-foot vessel that crews described as painted overall black with a white deckhouse. Reports from the *Enterprise* planes indicated, but were mistaken, that the Japanese had raised a white flag. Halsey had ordered the *Nashville* to take prisoners and then sink the ship. If the *Nashville* could not comply, then it was to sink the patrol ship first and then try to rescue any prisoners. Halsey cautioned the *Nashville*'s captain not to lose sight of the retreating task force that was now 18,000 yards away steaming at 25 knots towards Hawaii. However, the *Nashville*'s crew discovered the Japanese crew did not want to surrender and that they had not used a white flag. The cruiser went into action.

*Nashville*'s guns fired in anger at 1424. This time, gunnery was much improved. The *Nashville* moved closer to the target than its previous engagement with the *Nitto Maru* and positioned itself among the wave troughs to compensate for movement since the seas were still heavy. Still, the gun crews used 167 rounds to sink the second patrol craft at 1446. The ship sank at 36° 21' North latitude and 155° 14' East longitude. Halsey was also very disappointed with the performance of the *Enterprise*'s aircraft in their attempts to sink the patrol ships. He noted that more training was required. His aircraft expended 12,600 .50-caliber machine gun rounds, 800 .30-caliber machine gun bullets, 12 500-pound bombs, and 24 100-pound bombs to sink one, small vessel.

Recovery of the prisoners commenced and the *Nashville* gathered five Japanese seamen. The new prisoners of war indicated that there were eleven original crewmen on the patrol craft. With this action completed, the *Nashville* resumed course to rejoin the carriers and head home.

The first news of the Tokyo raid was an English language broadcast heard on the *Hornet* at 1445. The Japanese radio statement declared:

*Enemy bombers appeared over Tokyo today shortly after noon for the first time in the current East Asia War. Heavy and telling damage*

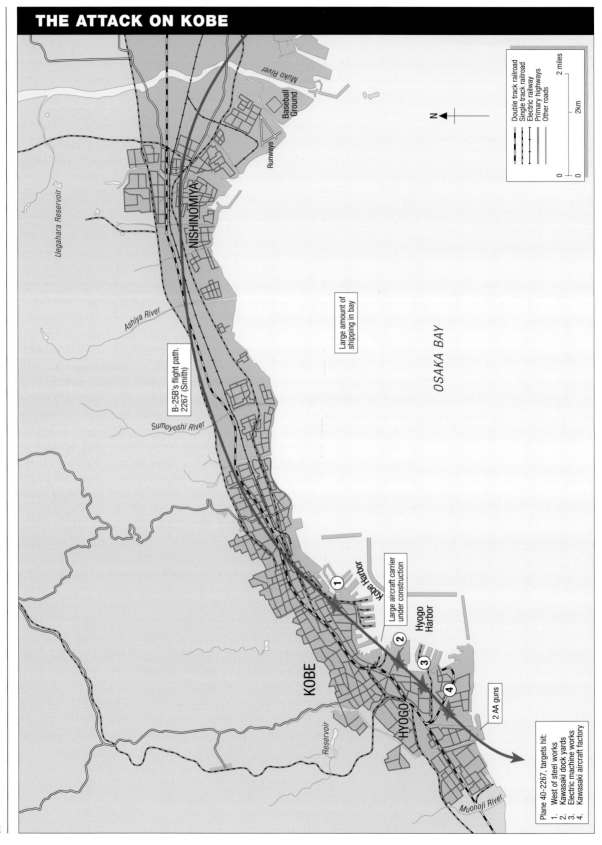

Double track railroad
Single track railroad
Electric railway
Primary highways
Other roads

N

0          2 miles
0      2km

Muko River

Baseball Ground

Runways

NISHINOMIYA

Uegahara Reservoir

Ashiya River

B-25B's flight path. 2267 (Smith)

Sumoyoshi River

Large amount of shipping in bay

OSAKA BAY

KOBE

Reservoir

Kobe Harbor

Large aircraft carrier under construction

Hyogo Harbor

HYOGO

2 AA guns

Muonoji River

Plane 40-2267, targets hit:

1.  West of steel works
2.  Kawasaki dock yards
3.  Electric machine works
4.  Kawasaki aircraft factory

*was inflicted on schools and hospitals, and the population shows much indignation.*

Undoubtedly, the Japanese did suffer collateral damage from the raid – how much can only be speculated. Curiously, a Japanese language report made a different statement, one more specific about the damage:

*A large fleet of heavy bombers appeared over Tokyo this noon and caused much damage to non-military objectives and some damage to factories. The known death toll is between three and four thousand so far. No planes were reported shot down over Tokyo. Osaka was also bombed. Tokyo reports several large fires burning.*

The rest of the voyage home was uneventful for the Navy's TF-16. It arrived in Pearl Harbor on the morning of April 25.

# THE FATE OF THE AIRCREWS: CRASHES, INTERNMENT, AND EXECUTION

All but one of the Doolittle aircraft involved in the raid crashed near or before their Chinese destinations, with the crews bailing out. York, despite Doolittle's admonitions, was forced to land in the Soviet Union where the Soviets interned the crew. Ten crews crashed in the interior of China, and four had to ditch in the East China Sea in the Chekiang Province. The landings in China and the support of Chinese people to return the downed crews incited Japanese retribution against thousands of innocent civilians. Japanese army units immediately hunted for the bomber crews in over 20,000 square miles for three months with revenge in mind. Chiang notified Roosevelt after the raid that the Japanese may have killed more than 250,000 civilians as a result and occupied more ground to eliminate China as a bomber staging area.

The longer flying distances, operational timing changes, and the failure to warn the Chinese landing strips resulted in the aircraft from the raid being lost. Poor flying weather over China also contributed significantly to the crew's failure to navigate there properly. Several crews reported that visibility was near zero. Failure to warn the Chinese landing sites meant no homing beacons, flares, and landing lights were set out for them. The crews' concern about fuel and range was somewhat muted since the aircraft escaping to China benefited from a strong 20 to 30 miles per hour tailwind. Doolittle also reported that when some of his B-25s flew over several airfields, the Chinese sounded air-raid warnings and turned off all landing lights. The multiple crash landings, bail-outs, and ditchings created problems for American and Chinese forces tasked with locating, gathering, and transporting downed crew members to Chungking and home. Many crew members had also suffered injuries that required extensive medical support. Three died during the landings. One crew member was killed when he bailed out and two others drowned when their plane ditched.

Doolittle and his crew were fortunate, as they bailed out about 70 miles north of Chuchow. He was able to contact a Chinese general

The Doolittle B-25B crews mostly came down in China and its waters, but one made it to the Soviet Union. Doolittle and his crew survived their crash landing. He was promoted to general officer after the raid. (US Navy)

officer from the Director of the Western Branch for Chekiang Province, who agreed to search for all of his remaining crews. Japanese claims about the raid emphasized the civilian damage and innocent lives lost. Tokyo radio broadcasts boasted that nine planes had now been shot down during the raid. Doolittle did not know the extent of damage that he had inflicted on the Japanese or the fate of his bomber force.

Sketchy reports from China reached Washington. Doolittle was able to send information to Arnold that indicated the raid surprised the Japanese, but that the raiding force was lost. Arnold's initial reaction to Roosevelt was mixed. In an April 21 memorandum to the President, he recognized the strategic impact of the raid, but was skeptical about the operation. Arnold's view was:

> *From the viewpoint of an Air Force operation the raid was not a success, for no raid is a success in which losses exceed ten percent and it now appears that probably all of the airplanes were lost.*

Still, Roosevelt and the country savored Doolittle's raid. Arnold's initial doubts revealed a tactical frame of mind and not a strategic one, but later memoranda attested to the raid's great value for morale and later shock to the Japanese military. Doolittle had been concerned about losing all of his planes from initial reports. He believed he would return to Washington a failure and face eventual courtmartial. His doubts were soon dismissed.

As crews were found and news of the raid spread, national leaders beamed with pride concerning America's first raid on Japan. Doolittle was elevated to one of America's first war heroes. He was immediately promoted to brigadier general a day after the raid and was later awarded the Congressional Medal of Honor. Arnold had earlier ordered all crew members to receive the Distinguished Flying Cross.

When the crews were transported to Chungking, they were decorated by the Chinese government. After this, they were sent to India and home.

The only crews not to make it home immediately were from the planes piloted by Farrow, Hallmark, and York. Farrow and Hallmark shared a common fate, landing in Japanese-occupied territory in China, and falling prisoner to the Japanese. The Japanese held the two crews, composed of eight members (two had drowned), in occupied Shanghai, but they were later transferred to Tokyo for about 46 days. In prison, they were interrogated and tortured to gain signed confessions alleging that Doolittle had attacked civilian targets on purpose. On June 18, the Japanese army sent the crews back to Shanghai and Kiangwan Military Prison to await trial.

Japanese military prosecutors started the trial on August 28. The unfortunate crews of the "Green Hornet" and "Bat out of Hell" were not given the opportunity to speak at the trial, nor able to offer any defense against charges that they had intentionally killed innocent women and children. The signed confessions, written in Japanese, sealed their fate. All of the crew members were sentenced to death. However, only Hallmark, Farrow, and Sgt Harold Spatz were executed, on October 15, 1942. The remaining five members were sentenced to life imprisonment. They all survived three years of brutal imprisonment except 2Lt Robert J. Meder who died due to malnutrition on December 1, 1943.

York's crew landed at a location in the Primorski province, about 25 miles north of Vladivostok in the USSR. Soviet military personnel inspected the plane upon its landing. York and his crew did not know what type of reception they would receive. Once they had identified themselves as "Americanski" they were well treated. The crew did not disclose their mission and tried to indicate to Soviet officials that they had come from Alaska, but their true mission was later discovered. Unfortunately, American diplomatic efforts failed to gain their release and they were interned; to add to the insult the American government had to pay 30,000 rubles per month for internment costs. The crew was sent to Okuna, three hundred miles south of Moscow, then to Okhansk

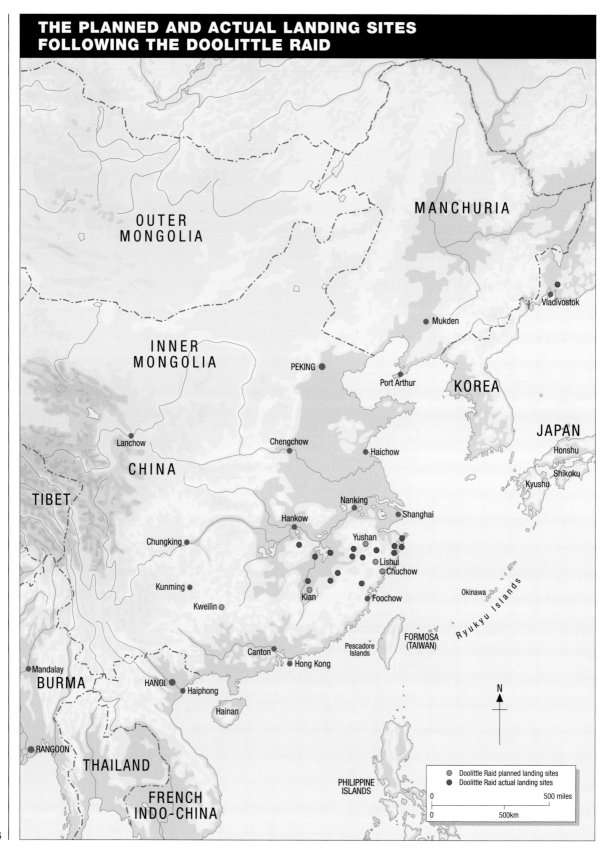

OUTER MONGOLIA

MANCHURIA

Vladivostok

Mukden

INNER MONGOLIA

PEKING

Port Arthur

KOREA

Lanchow

CHINA

Chengchow

Haichow

JAPAN

Honshu

Shikoku

Kyushu

TIBET

Nanking

Hankow

Chungking

Yushan

Shanghai

Lishui
Chuchow

Kunming

Kian

Foochow

Okinawa

Kweilin

Ryukyu Islands

Mandalay

Canton

Pescadore
Islands

FORMOSA
(TAIWAN)

BURMA

HANOI

Hong Kong

Haiphong

Hainan

N

RANGOON

THAILAND

FRENCH
INDO-CHINA

PHILIPPINE
ISLANDS

○ Doolittle Raid planned landing sites
● Doolittle Raid actual landing sites

0                          500 miles

0            500km

The Doolittle raid foreshadowed future US bombing missions against the Japanese home islands. In this 1945 photograph of the Tokyo area, one can see the area through which the crews had to navigate and select their targets. (Military History Institute).

on the western edge of Siberia. They later arrived in Central Asia. York bribed a guard who helped smuggle them over the Iranian border. Other Soviet guards, once the escape was detected, started to search for York's crew. York was able to find a British consulate, and they were offered sanctuary.

# AFTERMATH

The Doolittle Raid produced a profound psychological and military impact on both sides. With only 16 B-25s, Doolittle's calculated risk paid off handsomely in many strategic ways. It altered events in the Pacific Theater, with immediate effects on the war. The Japanese government, military, and people were pushed out of their security blanket of imagined invincibility created by its "Victory Disease" to the cold reality of fighting a determined foe. The Doolittle Raid demonstrated to the Japanese people that they were vulnerable to attack. After the Japanese press identified Jimmy Doolittle as the commander of the raid, they christened the bombing as "do-little" or "did-little." However, the "did-little" raid forced Japanese national leaders to alter their plans, and gave a welcome boost to American morale. The United States was able to change its strategic stance from a defensive to an offensive one, and showcased its military capability to all of the Axis powers.

The emperor and his military leadership were shocked that targets around the Imperial Palace were bombed. The raid embarrassed and humiliated the top army and navy leadership, especially Yamamoto. This action forced a major diversion of resources from further conquests to an attempt to annihilate the United States Pacific Fleet. Additionally, the Japanese military was forced to devote their limited resources to defending the home islands against any future aerial attack. For example, the IJN was forced to increase patrol and reconnaissance coverage while the army sent additional fighter units to defend Japan. The JAAF organized four fighter air groups, approximately 250 aircraft, to defend the home islands against future bombing raids. These actions deprived frontline units of vital fighter forces that would hinder offensive and defensive capabilities in the Southwest Pacific.

## MIDWAY: THE TURNING OF THE TIDE

One of the most profound changes to Japanese strategy was a switch from its defensive perimeter expansion in the Southwest Pacific area to concentration on the Central Pacific. IJN General Staff members had advocated advancement towards New Guinea. The objective was to sever any supply links between Australia and the United States. Instead, the fear of additional attacks on the emperor and other targets in Japan led planners to devise a two-front plan. They would continue to operate in the Southwest Pacific and move into the Solomon Islands and drive towards Port Moresby in New Guinea, after the American Navy had been neutralized. At a minimum, these proposed conquests would allow the Japanese to threaten at least the northern approaches to Australia. Future operations to take Samoa, Fiji, New Caledonia, and the New

Hebrides would provide bases to move further south to threaten other approaches towards Australia from America. This condition would allow the IJN and JAAF to isolate Australia from the United States from the east. Further Japanese movement south was dependent upon the destruction of the American carrier fleet.

The Japanese Army was likewise swayed to delay moving south to Australia. The army planned to participate with the IJN to extend its defensive boundaries to include Midway Island and perhaps further east to Hawaii. Army planners could intensify their campaign in the Southwest Pacific after the threat of the US Pacific Fleet was eliminated.

After the Doolittle Raid, the US Pacific Fleet now had five carriers in the theater: *Hornet, Enterprise, Lexington, Saratoga,* and *Yorktown.* If the IJN could meet the Americans in battle, their superior numbers in carriers could allow them to defeat the United States decisively and reduce any future carrier threat. Additionally, the Japanese had an opportunity to move directly upon Hawaii. If the United States faced isolation or capture of their Hawaiian military bases, then they would have to start any future operations from the West Coast or Alaska. This situation would create tremendous logistical and operational constraints for America. These conditions might seal a permanent victory for the empire.

Yamamoto had begun to design an offensive plan to defeat the Pacific Fleet and advance on Midway Island before the Doolittle Raid. Elements of Yamamoto's Combined Fleet had reservations about the plan. Still, the IJN's General Staff had agreed on the operation's principles by April 5, but had given little direction for the attack. After Doolittle's bombing, the General Staff could not stand in the way of the operation since they were also held responsible for the failure to protect the emperor. Opposition melted away and a strategic focus shifted from Australia to points east. Yamamoto's staff prepared a plan to take Midway. On May 5, Admiral Nagano Osami, Chief of the Japanese Navy's General Staff, approved Yamamoto's plan. Nagano's Imperial General Headquarters Navy Order Number 18 allowed Yamamoto to "carry out the occupation of Midway Island and key points in the western Aleutians in co-operation with the

Army." These actions allowed the Japanese to move closer to Hawaii and perhaps draw the Americans into combat. The attack on the Aleutians would become a diversion against the Americans. The provocative move towards Hawaii was calculated to draw out the American Pacific Fleet in a decisive battle and give the IJN an opportunity to destroy its nemesis.

A further demonstration of the threat to Japan's future military operations came at the battle of the Coral Sea. Japanese advancements in the Southwest Pacific were stymied, particular its move towards Port Moresby, by American carrier action. A combined American–Australian naval force had blunted the Japanese Port Moresby Invasion Group's thrust towards southern New Guinea. The IJN scored a tactical victory since the United States Navy lost the carrier *Lexington* while the Japanese only suffered the demise of a light carrier. However, the battle of the Coral Sea was a strategic victory for the Allies; the expansion of the Japanese was slowing and beginning to reverse. These activities only served to strengthen the Midway plan, now code-named Operation MI.

Midway would become the major turning point of the Pacific campaign. The United States would provide a crushing blow to the IJN's carrier forces and the Japanese would lose four major aircraft carriers. Their invasion of Midway was turned back and the taking of the western Aleutians a wasted effort; the Japanese war effort would move from the offensive to the defensive. The strategic naval balance would change forever with Midway, and the road to an Allied victory through conquest of territory held by the Japanese would be opened up.

Doolittle would continue to rise up the hierarchy of the AAF. He would gain commands in North Africa and Europe, and ended the war as a lieutenant general. (US Air Force)

# AMERICA ON THE MARCH

Roosevelt was ecstatic about the raid's results. The attack served his purpose of showing that America was capable of taking the offensive and that the Japanese were not indestructible. Tokyo's claims of unbroken success were debatable. Morale soared in the weeks after Roosevelt's April 21 announcement that the raid originated from a new base in "Shangri-La," a reference to a fictional location. He did not disclose any information about the *Hornet* or TF-16. Attacking the heart of Japan in payment for Pearl Harbor, at least partially, restored American honor.

However, the country could not afford to use its resources to mount another type of attack like the Doolittle Raid. This underscored efforts to build long-range bombers like the B-29. It did create uncertainty in the minds of Japanese national leadership as to where and when America would strike next. Doolittle's small raid forced many closed minds open, and Halsey proclaimed it "one of the most courageous deeds in all military history."

The raid also served other agendas. King had been a critic of the "Germany First" strategy. He had believed that the Japanese were the more important foes to fight. A loss in the Pacific meant a threat to Hawaii and the West Coast. Roosevelt's strategy was turned upside down, since the first strategic attack was on Japan instead of Germany. King demonstrated that America could win in the Pacific and that TF-16 and Doolittle had delivered the first major successful American raid in World War II.

Although delighted with the raid, there was some consternation within the War Department. Some Army planners argued that three of

The Doolittle Raid spurred America to increase its industrial production. The raid helped morale among the population in general, and industrial and military personnel in particular. From 1942 onwards, the nation became a key Allied manufacturing source for armaments and supplies that would support operations in all theaters of the war. (National Archives)

AAF bombers returned to Japan later in the war. B-29 aircraft attacked Kobe on June 20, 1945, dropping bombs near the original Doolittle target sites on Kobe's waterfront. (National Archives).

eight operational IJN carriers would send a retaliatory attack on the likes of Seattle or Los Angeles. Secretary of War Henry L. Stimson was very worried about the Japanese reaction. He discussed his angst with Chief of Staff General George C. Marshall concerning "the danger of a Jap attack on the West Coast." Army Headquarters G-2, Intelligence, feared that Japanese retribution would occur through carrier attacks on the West Coast. This concern was further amplified by Stimson's opinion that "having terribly lost face by this recent attack" the Japanese would "counterattack on us with carriers." The Japanese might also attack the Panama Canal, or try some other ingenious revenge plot. Marshall shored up defenses along the West Coast by sending additional air defense forces and ground forces. All of these measures added to the emphasis on the Pacific.

# REMEMBERING THE RAID TODAY

Seekers of historic sites connected with the Doolittle Raid will be somewhat disappointed. Most of the Japanese locations against which the raid was conducted have been razed due to AAF strategic bombing or to the normal consequences of post-war development. However, there are several historic and museum sites that have preserved the memory and artifacts of the raid. Many of those sites are spread throughout the United States. Some of the sites offer a broader context of the raid relative to the Pacific Campaign as a whole.

One of the sites related to the Doolittle Raid is the Lexington County Airport in Columbia, SC. The War Department expanded the facility in 1941 by increasing the length of the runways, building more facilities, infrastructure, and other support activities to improve the airport's ability to conduct military operations. In February 1942, Doolittle solicited volunteers from the 17th BG from this facility. Today, the site serves as the Columbia Metropolitan Airport. The airport is on the western outskirts of Columbia, the state capital of South Carolina, and is close to several interstates: I-20, I-26, and I-77.

The Doolittle Raiders' training area in Florida at Eglin Field is now Eglin Air Force Base (AFB). Eglin is host to the Air Force's Air Armaments Center, 33rd Fighter Wing, Air Force Research Laboratory – Munitions Directorate, and other tenant units. The base is located on the Florida panhandle and lies between Fort Walton Beach, on the Gulf of Mexico, and Niceville. The base is closed to the public. However, there is a large museum outside the main gate to the base. The Air Force Armament Museum focuses on a display of various bombs, missiles, rockets, and other munitions of interest to aviation enthusiasts. Admission is free and it is open daily, except for federal holidays. The museum is located between Highway 85 and State Road 189.

The Sacramento Air Depot in California, renamed McClellan AFB, is no longer an active military installation. It served the AAF and Air Force as a depot for major maintenance and logistics activities up until its closure in July 2001. The facility is open to the general public. The McClellan Aviation Museum is on the grounds of the former base. This museum contains exhibits on the Doolittle Raid and many aircraft displays. The displays contain many aircraft that served in the Cold War from the P-80B to an A-10A. Volunteers keep the museum open daily except for federal holidays. Access to McClellan AFB is gained from I-80 that runs through Sacramento, California's state capital.

Further west is the former site of Naval Air Station Alameda. The military facilities are now closed and the site is open to the public. Located on the eastern shore of San Francisco Bay, Alameda is west of Oakland and just south of the San Francisco–Oakland Bay Bridge near I-880 and I-80. The former naval air station is now home to the USS

*Hornet* Museum. Although CV-8, the *Hornet* that launched the Doolittle Raid, was lost in 1942, this museum covers a wide range of US naval history. The museum is housed on CV-12, a replacement for CV-8. CV-12 served through World War II and until 1970. It recovered returning Apollo 11 and 12 astronauts.

The last major staging area that visitors can view is Pearl Harbor. The naval base at Pearl Harbor, near Honolulu, HI is still an active military installation. Like Eglin AFB, access to many parts of the base is restricted for the general public. However, individuals can visit several interesting sites while at Pearl Harbor. Pearl Harbor is easily reached off the H-1 freeway. The USS *Arizona* Memorial provides a free tour of the remnants of the ship and puts into context the events of the early Pacific war. Next door is the USS *Bowfin*, a World War II submarine. The newest addition to Pearl Harbor is the USS *Missouri*, a battleship veteran of many Pacific campaigns and site of the Japanese unconditional surrender on September 2, 1945. One can move from the beginning of the United States' involvement in the Pacific War to its end in this one location.

The damage caused by military action, explosive population growth after the war, and development has changed the face of Japan. Although major landmarks such as the Imperial Palace remain in Tokyo, there are not many visible sites of the raid. Individuals can still enter Tokyo Bay and see many of the major areas where the B-25s flew over and conducted bombing raids. Yokosuka is now, ironically, a major United States naval base for the Pacific Fleet. Similar to other active United States military installations, this facility is closed to the public. However, one can view much of Yokosuka from the shoreline. Much of the waterfront around Tokyo Bay, Kobe, and Nagoya has also changed due to modernization and redevelopment.

# BIBLIOGRAPHY

Assistant Chief of Staff Intelligence, *Report of the Doolittle Raid, 18 April 1942* (located on microfilm roll A1250 at the Air Force Historical Research Agency, Maxwell AFB, AL) (declassified)

Assistant Chief of Staff Intelligence, *Tokyo Raid Material 1942* (located on microfilm roll A1289 at the Air Force Historical Research Agency, Maxwell AFB, AL) (declassified)

Stetson Conn, Rose C. Engleman and Byron Fairchild, *Guarding the United States and Its Outposts* (Washington, DC: Center of Military History, 1989)

Alvin D. Cox, "Strategic Bombing in the Pacific, 1942–1945" in *Case Studies in Strategic Bombardment*, ed. R. Cargill Hall (Washington, DC: Air Force History and Museums Program, 1998)

F.S. Craven, *Report of Sinking of Two Enemy Patrol Boats on 18 April 1942* (USS *Nashville*: April 21, 1942) (declassified)

James H. Doolittle, *I Could Never Be So Lucky Again* (New York: Bantam Books, 1991)

Carroll V. Glines, *The Doolittle Raid* (New York: Orion Books, 1988)

Carroll V. Glines, *Doolittle's Tokyo Raiders* (Princeton, NJ: Van Nostrand, 1964)

Charles R. Greening, *The First Joint Action* (Norfolk, VA: Armed Forces Staff College, December 21, 1948) (declassified)

William F. Halsey, *Report of Action in Connection with the Bombing of Tokyo on April 18, 1942* (Zero Minus Ten) Serial 088, (April 24, 1942) (declassified)

Headquarters, USAFE and Eighth Army (Rear), *Homeland Air Defense Operations Record Japanese Monograph 157* (undated)

Headquarters, USAFE and Eighth Army (Rear), *Homeland Operations Record Japanese Monograph 17* (undated)

John W. Huston, *American Airpower Comes of Age: General Henry H. "Hap" Arnold's World War II Diaries* (Maxwell AFB, AL: Air University Press, 2002)

Military Analysis Division, *United States Strategic Bombing Survey (Pacific): Japanese Air Power* (July 1946)

Military History Section, *Homeland Defense Naval Operations December 1941–March 1943, Part I, Japanese Monograph 109* (Tokyo: Headquarters, Army Forces Far East, March 24, 1953)

Marc A. Mitscher, *Report of Action, April 18, 1942, With Notable Events Prior and Subsequent Thereto*, Serial 0015, (USS *Hornet*, April 28, 1942, declassified)

Samuel Eliot Morison, *History of United States Naval Operations in World War II.* Volume III: *The Rising Sun in the Pacific 1931–April 1942* (Boston: Little, Brown and Company, 1955)

G.D. Murray, *Report of Action in Connection with the Bombing of Tokyo on April 18, 1942* (Zero Minus Ten) Serial 088, (USS *Enterprise*, April 23, 1942, declassified)

Craig Nelson, *The First Heroes* (New York: Viking, 2002)

Chester W. Nimitz, *Report of Action in Connection with the Bombing of Tokyo on April 18, 1942*, CINCPAC File No. A16(4)/(01) (May 4, 1942, declassified)

E.B. Potter, *Nimitz* (Annapolis, MD: Naval Institute Press, 1976)

E.B. Potter, *Seapower* (Annapolis, MD: Naval Institute Press, 1981)

Duane Schultz, *The Doolittle Raid* (New York: St. Martin's Press, 1988)

Michael S. Sherry, *The Rise of American Air Power: The Creation of Armageddon* (New Haven, CT: Yale University Press, 1987)

Paul H. Silverstone, *US Warships of World War II* (Garden City, NY: Doubleday, 1965)

Ronald H. Spector, *Eagle Against the Sun* (New York: Vintage, 1985)

Task Force Sixteen, *US Pacific Fleet War Diary April 1, 1942 to April 30, 1942*, A12-1 Serial 0025 (declassified)

# INDEX